OLD MO

HOROSCOPE AND ASTRAL DIARY

ARIES

OLD MOORE'S

HOROSCOPE AND ASTRAL DIARY

ARIES

foulsham
LONDON • NEW YORK • TORONTO • SYDNEY

foulsham

Capital Point, 33 Bath Road, Slough, Berkshire, SL1 3UF, England

Foulsham books can be found in all good bookshops and direct from www.foulsham.com

ISBN: 978-0-572-03652-2

Printed in Great Britain by Cox & Wyman Ltd, Reading, Berkshire.

CONTENTS

INTRODUCTION

A strology has been with us for a very long time and our fascination for the starry heavens seems to go back many thousands of years. Incised bones carrying lunar calendars have been found that are tens of thousands of years old, and our belief that the stars and planets have a bearing on our daily lives could easily be almost as ancient. Astrology was studied in all the major civilisations, and shows no signs of diminishing in popularity in the 21st century. Old Moore, a time-served veteran in astrological research, continues to monitor the zodiac and has produced the Astral Diary for 2012, tailor-made to your own astrological make-up.

Old Moore's Astral Diary is unique in its ability to get the heart of your nature and to offer you the sort of advice that might come from a trusted friend. The Diaries are structured in such a way that you can see in a day-by-day sense exactly how the planets are working for you. The diary section advises how you can get the best from upcoming situations and allows you to plan ahead successfully. There is room in the daily sections to put your own observations or even appointments, and the book is conveniently structured to stay with you throughout the year.

Whilst other popular astrology books merely deal with your astrological Sun sign, the Astral Diaries go much further. Every person on the planet is unique, and Old Moore allows you to access your individuality in a number of ways. The front section gives you the chance to work out the placement of the Moon at the time of your birth and to see how its position has set an important seal on your overall nature. Perhaps most important of all, you can use the Astral Diary to discover your Rising sign. This is the zodiac sign that was appearing over the Eastern horizon at the time of your birth, and is just as important to you as an individual as is your Sun sign.

It is the synthesis of many different astrological possibilities that makes you what you are, and with the Astral Diaries you can learn so much. How do you react to love and romance? Through the unique Venus tables and the readings that follow them, you can learn where the planet Venus was at the time of your birth. It is even possible to register when little Mercury is 'retrograde', which means that it appears to be moving backwards in space when viewed from the Earth. Mercury rules communication, so be prepared to deal with a few setbacks in this area when you see the sign ☿. The Astral Diary will be an interest and a support throughout the whole year ahead.

Old Moore extends his customary greeting to all people of the Earth and offers his age-old wishes for a happy and prosperous period ahead.

THE ESSENCE OF ARIES

Exploring the Personality of Aries the Ram

(21st MARCH – 20th APRIL)

What's in a sign?

Aries is not the first sign of the zodiac by accident. It's the place in the year when the spring begins, and so it represents some of the most dynamic forces in nature, and within the zodiac as a whole. As a result the very essence of your nature is geared towards promoting yourself in life and pushing your ideas forward very positively. You don't brook a great deal of interference in your life, but you are quite willing to help others as much as you can, provided that to do so doesn't curb your natural desire to get on in life.

Aries people are not universally liked, though your true friends remain loyal to you under almost any circumstances. But why should it be that such a dynamic and go-getting person does meet with some opposition? The answer is simple: not everyone is quite so sure of themselves as you are and many tend to get nervous when faced with the sheer power of the Aries personality. If there is one factor within your own control that could counter these problems it is the adoption of some humility – that commodity which is so important for you to dredge from the depths of your nature. If you only show the world that you are human, and that you are well aware of the fact, most people would follow you willingly to the very gates of hell. The most successful Aries subjects know this fact and cultivate it to the full.

Your executive skills are never in doubt and you can get almost anything practical done whilst others are still jumping from foot to foot. That's why you are such a good organiser and are so likely to be out there at the front of any venture. Adventurous and quite willing to show your bravery in public, you can even surprise yourself sometimes with the limits you are likely to go to in order to reach solutions that seem right to you.

Kind to those you take to, you can be universally loved when working at your best. Despite this there will be times in your life when you simply can't understand why some people just don't like you. Maybe there's an element of jealousy involved.

Aries resources

The part of the zodiac occupied by the sign of Aries has, for many centuries, been recognised as the home of self-awareness. This means that there isn't a person anywhere else in the zodiac that has a better knowledge of self than you do. But this isn't necessarily an intellectual process with Aries, more a response to the very blood that is coursing through your veins. Aries' success doesn't so much come from spending hours working out the pros and cons of any given course of action, more from the thrill of actually getting stuck in. If you find yourself forced into a life that means constantly having to think everything through to the tiniest detail, there is likely to be some frustration in evidence.

Aries is ruled by Mars, arguably the most go-getting of all the planets in the solar system. Mars is martial and demands practical ways of expressing latent power. It also requires absolute obedience from subordinates. When this is forthcoming, Aries individuals are the most magnanimous people to be found anywhere. Loyalty is not a problem and there have been many instances in history when Aries people were quite willing to die for their friends if necessary.

When other people are willing to give up and go with the flow, you will still be out there pitching for the result that seems most advantageous to you. It isn't something you can particularly control and those who don't know you well could find you sometimes curt and over-demanding as a result. But because you are tenacious you can pick the bones out of any situation and will usually arrive at your desired destination, if you don't collapse with fatigue on the way.

Routines, or having to take life at the pace of less motivated types, won't suit you at all. Imprisonment of any sort, even in a failed relationship, is sheer torture and you will move heaven and earth to get out into the big, wide world, where you can exploit your natural potential to the full. Few people know you really well because you don't always explain yourself adequately. The ones who do adore you.

Beneath the surface

Whereas some zodiac signs are likely to spend a great deal of their lives looking carefully at the innermost recesses of their own minds, Aries individuals tend to prefer the cut and thrust of the practical world. Aries people are not natural philosophers, but that doesn't mean that you aren't just as complicated beneath the surface as any of your astrological brothers and sisters. So what is it that makes the Aries firebrand think and act in the way that it does? To a great extent it is a lack of basic self-confidence.

This statement might seem rather odd, bearing in mind that a fair percentage of the people running our world were born under the sign of the Ram, but it is true nevertheless. Why? Because people who know themselves and their capabilities really well don't feel the constant need to prove themselves in the way that is the driving force of your zodiac sign. Not that your naturally progressive tendencies are a fault. On the contrary, if used correctly they can help you to create a much better, fairer and happier world, at least in your own vicinity.

The fact that you occasionally take your ball and go home if you can't get your own way is really down to the same insecurity that is noticeable through many facets of your nature. If Aries can't rule, it often doesn't want to play at all. A deep resentment and a brooding quality can build up in the minds and souls of some thwarted Aries types, a tendency that you need to combat. Better by far to try and compromise, itself a word that doesn't exist in the vocabularies of the least enlightened people born under the sign of the Ram. Once this lesson is learned, inner happiness increases and you relax into your life much more.

The way you think about others is directly related to the way you consider they think about you. This leads to another surprising fact regarding the zodiac sign. Aries people absolutely hate to be disliked, though they would move heaven and earth to prove that this isn't the case. And as a result Aries both loves and hates with a passion. Deep inside you can sometimes be a child shivering in the dark. If you only realise this fact your path to happiness and success is almost assured. Of course to do so takes a good deal of courage – but that's a commodity you don't lack.

Making the best of yourself

It would be quite clear to any observer that you are not the sort of person who likes to hang around at the back of a queue, or who would relish constantly taking orders from people who may not know situations as well as you do. For that reason alone you are better in positions that see you out there at the front, giving commands and enjoying the cut and thrust of everyday life. In a career sense this means that whatever you do you are happiest telling those around you how to do it too. Many Aries people quite naturally find their way to the top of the tree and don't usually have too much trouble staying there.

It is important to remember, however, that there is another side to your nature: the giving qualities beneath your natural dominance. You can always be around when people need you the most, encouraging and even gently pushing when it is necessary. By keeping friends and being willing to nurture relationships across a broad spectrum, you gradually get to know what makes those around you tick. This makes for a more patient and understanding sort of Aries subject – the most potent of all.

Even your resilience is not endless, which is why it is important to remember that there are times when you need rest. Bearing in mind that you are not superhuman is the hardest lesson to learn, but the admission brings humility, something that Aries needs to cultivate whenever possible.

Try to avoid living a restricted life and make your social contacts frequent and important. Realise that there is much more to life than work and spend some of your free time genuinely attempting to help those who are less well off than you are. Crucially you must remember that 'help' is not the same as domination.

The impressions you give

This section may well be of less interest to Aries subjects than it would be to certain other zodiac signs. The reason is quite clear. Aries people are far less interested in what others think about them than almost anyone else – or at least they tell themselves that they are. Either way it is counterproductive to ignore the opinions of the world at large because to do so creates stumbling blocks, even in a practical sense.

Those around you probably find you extremely capable and well able to deal with almost any situation that comes your way. Most are willing to rely heavily on you and the majority would almost instinctively see you as a leader. Whether or not they like you at the same time is really dependent on the way you handle situations. That's the difference between the go-getting, sometimes selfish type of Aries subject and the more enlightened amongst this illustrious sign.

You are viewed as being exciting and well able to raise enthusiasm for almost any project that takes your fancy. Of course this implies a great responsibility because you are always expected to come up with the goods. The world tends to put certain people on a pedestal, and you are one of them. On the other side of the coin we are all inclined to fire arrows at the elevated, so maintaining your position isn't very easy.

Most of the time you are seen as being magnanimous and kind, factors that you can exploit, whilst at the same time recognising the depth of the responsibility that comes with being an Aries subject. It might not be a bad thing to allow those around you to see that you too have feet of clay. This will make them respect and support you all the more, and even Aries people really do need to feel loved. A well-balanced Aries subject is one of the most elevated spirits to be found anywhere.

The way forward

You certainly enjoy life more when looking at it from the top of the tree. Struggling to get by is not in the least interesting to your zodiac sign and you can soon become miserable if things are not going well for you. That's why it is probably quite justified in your case to work tenaciously in order to achieve your objectives. Ideally, once you have realised some sort of success and security for yourself, you should then be willing to sit and watch life go by a little more. In fact this doesn't happen. The reason for this is clear. The

Aries subject who learns how to succeed rarely knows when to stop – it's as simple as that.

Splitting your life into different components can help, if only because this means that you don't get the various elements mixed up. So, for example, don't confuse your love life with your professional needs, or your family with colleagues. This process allows you to view life in manageable chunks and also makes it possible for you to realise when any one of them may be working well. As a result you will put the effort where it's needed, and enjoy what is going well for you.

If you want to know real happiness you will also have to learn that acquisition for its own sake brings hollow rewards at best. When your talents are being turned outward to the world at large, you are one of the most potent and successful people around. What is more you should find yourself to be a much happier person when you are lending a hand to the wider world. This is possible, maybe outside of your normal professional sphere, though even where voluntary work is concerned it is important not to push yourself to the point of fatigue.

Keep yourself physically fit, without necessarily expecting that you can run to the South Pole and back, and stay away from too many stimulants, such as alcohol and nicotine. The fact is that you are best when living a healthy life, but it doesn't help either if you make even abstinence into an art form. Balance is important, as is moderation – itself a word that is difficult for you to understand. In terms of your approach to other people it's important to realise that everyone has a specific point of view. These might be different to yours, but they are not necessarily wrong. Sort out the friends who are most important to you and stick with them, whilst at the same time realising that almost everyone can be a pal – with just a little effort.

ARIES ON THE CUSP

Old Moore is often asked how astrological profiles are altered for those people born at either the beginning or the end of a zodiac sign, or, more properly, on the cusps of a sign. In the case of Aries this would be on the 21st of March and for two or three days after, and similarly at the end of the sign, probably from the 18th to the 20th of April. In this year's Astral Diaries, once again, Old Moore sets out to explain the differences regarding cuspid signs.

The Pisces Cusp – March 21st to March 24th

With the Sun so close to the zodiac sign of Pisces at the time you were born, it is distinctly possible that you have always had some doubts when reading a character breakdown written specifically for the sign of Aries. This isn't surprising because no zodiac sign has a definite start or end, they merely merge together. As a result there are some of the characteristics of the sign of the Fishes that are intermingled with the qualities of Aries in your nature.

What we probably find, as a result, is a greater degree of emotional sensitivity and a tendency to be more cognisant of what the rest of humanity is feeling. This is not to imply that Aries is unfeeling, but rather that Pisceans actively make humanity their business.

You are still able to achieve your most desired objectives in the practical world, but on the way, you stop to listen to the heartbeat of the planet on which you live. A very good thing, of course, but at the same time there is some conflict created if your slightly dream-like tendencies get in the way of your absolute need to see things through to their logical conclusion.

Nobody knows you better than you know yourself, or at least that's what the Aries qualities within you say, but that isn't always verified by some of the self-doubt that comes from the direction of the Fishes. As in all matters astrological, a position of balance has to be achieved in order to reconcile the differing qualities of your nature. In your case, this is best accomplished by being willing to stop and think once in a while and by refusing to allow your depth to be a problem.

Dealt with properly, the conjoining of Pisces and Aries can be a wondrous and joyful affair, a harmony of opposites that always makes you interesting to know. Your position in the world is naturally one of authority but at the same time you need to serve. That's why some people with this sort of mixture of astrological qualities would make such good administrators in a hospital, or in any position where the alternate astrological needs are well balanced. In the chocolate box of life you are certainly a 'soft centre'.

The Taurus Cusp – April 18th to April 20th

The merge from Aries to Taurus is much less well defined than the one at the other side of Aries, but it can be very useful to you all the same. Like the Pisces-influenced Aries you may be slightly more quiet than would be the case with the Ram taken alone and your thought processes are probably not quite as fast. But to compensate for this fact you don't rush into things quite as much and are willing to allow ideas to mature more fully.

Your sense of harmony and beauty is strong and you know, in a very definite way, exactly what you want. As a result your home will be distinctive but tasteful and it's a place where you need space to be alone sometimes, which the true Aries subject probably does not. You do not lack the confidence to make things look the way you want them, but you have a need to display these things to the world at large and sometimes even to talk about how good you are at decoration and design.

If anyone finds you pushy, it is probably because they don't really know what makes you tick. Although you are willing to mix with almost anyone, you are more inclined, at base, to have a few very close friends who stay at the forefront of your life for a long time. It is likely that you enjoy refined company and you wouldn't take kindly to the dark, the sordid, or the downright crude in life.

Things don't get you down as much as can sometimes be seen to be the case for Taurus when taken alone and you are rarely stumped for a progressive and practical idea when one is needed most. At all levels, your creative energy is evident and some of you even have the ability to make this into a business, since Aries offers the practical and administrative spark that Taurus can sometimes lack.

In matters of love, you are ardent and sincere, probably an idealist, and you know what you want in a partner. Whilst this is also true in the case of Taurus, you are different, because you are much more likely, not only to look, but also to say something about the way you feel.

Being naturally friendly you rarely go short of the right sort of help and support when it is most vital. Part of the reason for this lies in the fact that you are so willing to be the sounding-board for the concerns of your friends. All in all you can be very contented with your lot, but you never stop searching for something better all the same. At its best, this is one of the most progressive cuspal matches of them all.

ARIES AND ITS ASCENDANTS

The nature of every individual on the planet is composed of the rich variety of zodiac signs and planetary positions that were present at the time of their birth. Your Sun sign, which in your case is Aries, is one of the many factors when it comes to assessing the unique person you are. Probably the most important consideration, other than your Sun sign, is to establish the zodiac sign that was rising over the eastern horizon at the time that you were born. This is your Ascending or Rising sign. Most popular astrology fails to take account of the Ascendant, and yet its importance remains with you from the very moment of your birth, through every day of your life. The Ascendant is evident in the way you approach the world, and so, when meeting a person for the first time, it is this astrological influence that you are most likely to notice first. Our Ascending sign essentially represents what we appear to be, while our Sun sign is what we feel inside ourselves.

The Ascendant also has the potential for modifying our overall nature. For example, if you were born at a time of day when Aries was passing over the eastern horizon (this would be around the time of dawn) then you would be classed as a double Aries. As such you would typify this zodiac sign, both internally and in your dealings with others. However, if your Ascendant sign turned out to be a Water sign, such as Pisces, there would be a profound alteration of nature, away from the expected qualities of Aries.

One of the reasons that popular astrology often ignores the Ascendant is that it has always been rather difficult to establish. Old Moore has found a way to make this possible by devising an easy-to-use table, which you will find on page 159 of this book. Using this, you can establish your Ascendant sign at a glance. You will need to know your rough time of birth, then it is simply a case of following the instructions.

For those readers who have no idea of their time of birth it might be worth allowing a good friend, or perhaps your partner, to read through the section that follows this introduction. Someone who deals with you on a regular basis may easily discover your Ascending sign, even though you could have some difficulty establishing it for yourself. A good understanding of this component of your nature is essential if you want to be aware of that 'other person' who is responsible for the way you make contact with the world at large. Your Sun sign, Ascendant sign, and the other pointers in this book will, together, allow you a far better understanding of what makes you tick as an individual. Peeling back the different layers of your astrological make-up can be an enlightening experience, and the Ascendant may represent one of the most important layers of all.

Aries with Aries Ascendant

What you see is what you get with this combination. You typify the no-nonsense approach of Aries at its best. All the same this combination is quite daunting when viewed through the eyes of other, less dominant sorts of people. You tend to push your way though situations that would find others cowering in a corner and you are afraid of very little. With a determination to succeed that makes you a force to be reckoned with, you leave the world in no doubt as to your intentions and tend to be rather too brusque for your own good on occasions.

At heart you are kind and loving, able to offer assistance to the downtrodden and sad, and usually willing to take on board the cares of people who have a part to play in your life. No-one would doubt your sincerity, or your honesty, though you may utilise slightly less than orthodox ways of getting your own way on those occasions when you feel you have right on your side. You are a loving partner and a good parent, though where children are concerned you tend to be rather too protective. The trouble is that you know what a big, bad world it can be and probably feel that you are better equipped to deal with things than anyone else.

Aries with Taurus Ascendant

This is a much quieter combination, so much so that even experienced astrologers would be unlikely to recognise you as an Aries subject at all, unless of course they came to know you very well. Your approach to life tends to be quiet and considered and there is a great danger that you could suppress those feelings that others of your kind would be only too willing to verbalise. To compensate you are deeply creative and will think matters through much more readily than more dominant Aries types would be inclined to do. Reaching out towards the world, you are, nevertheless, somewhat locked inside yourself and can struggle to achieve the level of communication that you so desperately need. Frustration might easily follow, were it not for the fact that you possess a quiet determination that, to those in the know, is the clearest window through to your Aries soul.

The care for others is stronger here than with almost any other Aries type and you certainly demonstrate this at all levels. The fact is that you live a great percentage of your life in service to the people you take to, whilst at the same time being able to shut the door firmly in the face of people who irritate or anger you. You are deeply motivated towards family relationships.

Aries with Gemini Ascendant

A fairly jolly combination this, though by no means easy for others to come to terms with. You fly about from pillar to post and rarely stop long enough to take a breath. Admittedly this suits your own needs very well, but it can be a source of some disquiet to those around you, since they may not possess your energy or motivation. Those who know you well are deeply in awe of your capacity to keep going long after almost everyone else would have given up and gone home, though this quality is not always as wonderful as it sounds because it means that you put more pressure on your nervous system than just about any other astrological combination.

You need to be mindful of your nervous system, which responds to the erratic, mercurial quality of Gemini. Problems only really arise when the Aries part of you makes demands that the Gemini component finds difficult to deal with. There are paradoxes galore here and some of them need sorting out if you are ever fully to understand yourself, or are to be in a position when others know what makes you tick.

In relationships you might be a little fickle, but you are a real charmer and never stuck for the right words, no matter who you are dealing with. Your tenacity knows no bounds, though perhaps it should!

Aries with Cancer Ascendant

The main problem that you experience in life shows itself as a direct result of the meshing of these two very different zodiac signs. At heart Aries needs to dominate, whereas Cancer shows a desire to nurture. All too often the result can be a protective arm that is so strong that nobody could possibly get out from under it. Lighten your own load, and that of those you care for, by being willing to sit back and watch others please themselves a little. You might think that you know best, and your heart is clearly in the right place, but try to realise what life is like when someone is always on hand to tell you that they know better then you do.

But in a way this is a little severe, because you are fairly intuitive and your instincts would rarely lead you astray. Nobody could ask for a better partner or parent than you, though they might request a slightly less attentive one. In matters of work you are conscientious and are probably best suited to a job that means sorting out the kind of mess that humanity is so good at creating. You probably spend your spare time untangling balls of wool, though you are quite sporting too and could easily make the Olympics. Once there you would not win however, because you would be too concerned about all the other competitors.

Aries with Leo Ascendant

Here we come upon the first situation of Aries being allied with another Fire sign. This creates a character that could appear to be typically Aries at first sight and in many ways it is, though there are subtle differences that should not be ignored. Although you have the typical Aries ability to get things done, many of the tasks you do undertake will be for and on behalf of others. You can be proud, and on some occasions even haughty, and yet you are also regal in your bearing and honest to the point of absurdity. Nobody could doubt your sincerity and you have the soul of a poet combined with the courage of a lion.

All this is good, but it makes you rather difficult to approach, unless the person in question has first adopted a crouching and subservient attitude although you would not wish them to do so. It's simply that the impression you give and the motivation that underpins it are two quite different things. You are greatly respected and in the case of those individuals who know your real nature, you are also deeply loved. But life would be much simpler if you didn't always have to fight the wars that those around you are happy to start. Relaxation is a word that you don't really understand and you would do yourself a favour if you looked it up in a dictionary.

Aries with Virgo Ascendant

Virgo is steady and sure, though also fussy and stubborn. Aries is fast and determined, restless and active. It can already be seen that this is a rather strange meeting of characteristics and because Virgo is ruled by the capricious Mercury, the ultimate result will change from hour to hour and day to day. It isn't merely that others find it difficult to know where they are with you, they can't even understand what makes you tick. This will make you the subject of endless fascination and attention, at which you will be apparently surprised but inwardly pleased. If anyone ever really gets to know what goes on in that busy mind they may find the implications very difficult to deal with and it is a fact that only you would have the ability to live inside your crowded head.

As a partner and a parent you are second to none, though you tend to get on better with your children once they start to grow, since by this time you may be slightly less restricting to their own desires, which will often clash with your own on their behalf. You are capable of give and take and could certainly not be considered selfish, though your constant desire to get the best from everyone might occasionally be misconstrued.

Aries with Libra Ascendant

Libra has the tendency to bring out the best in any zodiac sign, and this is no exception when it comes together with Aries. You may, in fact, be the most comfortable of all Aries types, simply because Libra tempers some of your more assertive qualities and gives you the chance to balance out opposing forces, both inside yourself and in the world outside. You are fun to be with and make the staunchest friend possible. Although you are generally affable, few people would try to put one over on you, because they would quickly come to know how far you are willing to go before you let forth a string of invective that would shock those who previously underestimated your basic Aries traits.

Home and family are very dear to you, but you are more tolerant than some Aries types are inclined to be and you have a youthful zest for life that should stay with you no matter what age you manage to achieve. There is always something interesting to do and your mind is a constant stream of possibilities. This makes you very creative and you may also demonstrate a desire to look good at all times. You may not always be quite as confident as you appear to be, but few would guess the fact.

Aries with Scorpio Ascendant

The two very different faces of Mars come together in this potent, magnetic and quite awe-inspiring combination. Your natural inclination is towards secrecy and this fact, together with the natural attractions of the sensual Scorpio nature, makes you the object of great curiosity. This means that you will not go short of attention and should ensure that you are always being analysed by people who may never get to know you at all. At heart you prefer your own company, and yet life appears to find means to push you into the public gaze time and again. Most people with this combination ooze sex appeal and can use this fact as a stepping stone to personal success, yet without losing any integrity or loosening the cords of a deeply moralistic nature.

On those occasions when you do lose your temper, there isn't a character in the length and breadth of the zodiac who would have either the words or the courage to stand against the stream of invective that follows. On really rare occasions you might even scare yourself. As far as family members are concerned a simple look should be enough to show when you are not amused. Few people are left unmoved by your presence in their life.

Aries with Sagittarius Ascendant

What a lovely combination this can be, for the devil-may-care aspects of Sagittarius lighten the load of a sometimes too-serious Aries interior. Everything that glistens is not gold, though it's hard to convince you of the fact because, to mix metaphors, you can make a silk purse out of a sow's ear. Almost everyone loves you and in return you offer a friendship that is warm and protective, but not as demanding as sometimes tends to be the case with the Aries type. Relationships may be many and varied and there is often more than one major attachment in the life of those holding this combination. You will bring a breath of spring to any attachment, though you need to ensure that the person concerned is capable of keeping up with the hectic pace of your life.

It may appear from time to time that you are rather too trusting for your own good, though deep inside you are very astute and it seems that almost everything you undertake works out well in the end. This has nothing to do with native luck and is really down to the fact that you are much more calculating than might appear to be the case at first sight. As a parent you are protective yet offer sufficient room for self-expression.

Aries with Capricorn Ascendant

If ever anyone could be accused of setting off immediately, but slowly, it has to be you. These are very contradictory signs and the differences will express themselves in a variety of ways. One thing is certain, you have tremendous tenacity and will see a job through patiently from beginning to end, without tiring on the way, and ensuring that every detail is taken care of properly. This combination often bestows good health and a great capacity for continuity, particularly in terms of the length of life. You are certainly not as argumentative as the typical Aries, but you do know how to get your own way, which is just as well because you are usually thinking on behalf of everyone else and not just on your own account.

At home you can relax, which is a blessing for Aries, though in fact you seldom choose to do so because you always have some project or other on the go. You probably enjoy knocking down and rebuilding walls, though this is a practical tendency and not responsive to relationships, in which you are ardent and sincere. Impetuosity is as close to your heart as is the case for any type of Aries subject, though you certainly have the ability to appear patient and steady. But it's just a front, isn't it?

Aries with Aquarius Ascendant

The person standing on a soap box in the corner of the park, extolling the virtues of this or that, could quite easily be an Aries with an Aquarian Ascendant. You are certainly not averse to speaking your mind and you have plenty to talk about because you are the best social reformer and political animal of them all. Unorthodox in your approach, you have the ability to keep everyone guessing, except when it comes to getting your own way, for in this nobody doubts your natural abilities. You can put theories into practice very well and on the way you retain a sense of individuality that would shock more conservative types. It's true that a few people might find you a little difficult to approach and this is partly because you have an inner reserve and strength which is difficult for others to fathom.

In the world at large you take your place at the front, as any good Arian should, and yet you offer room for others to share your platform. You keep up with the latest innovations and treat family members as the genuine friends that you believe them to be. Care needs to be taken when picking a life partner, for you are an original, and not just anyone could match the peculiarities thrown up by this astrological combination.

Aries with Pisces Ascendant

Although not an easy combination to deal with, the Aries with a Piscean Ascendant does, nevertheless, bring something very special to the world in the way of natural understanding allied to practical assistance. It's true that you can sometimes be a dreamer, but there is nothing wrong with that as long as you have the ability to turn some of your wishes into reality, and this you are easily able to do, usually for the sake of those around you. Conversation comes easily to you, though you also possess a slightly wistful and poetic side to your nature, which is attractive to the many people who call you a friend. A natural entertainer, you bring a sense of the comic to the often serious qualities of Aries, though without losing the determination that typifies the sign.

In relationships you are ardent, sincere and supportive, with a strong social conscience that sometimes finds you fighting the battles of the less privileged members of society. Family is important to you and this is a combination that invariably leads to parenthood. Away from the cut and thrust of everyday life you relax more fully and think about matters more deeply than more typical Aries types might.

THE MOON AND THE PART IT PLAYS IN YOUR LIFE

In astrology the Moon is probably the single most important heavenly body after the Sun. Its unique position, as partner to the Earth on its journey around the solar system, means that the Moon appears to pass through the signs of the zodiac extremely quickly. The zodiac position of the Moon at the time of your birth plays a great part in personal character and is especially significant in the build-up of your emotional nature.

Sun Moon Cycles

The first lunar cycle deals with the part the position of the Moon plays relative to your Sun sign. I have made the fluctuations of this pattern easy for you to understand by means of a simple cyclic graph. It appears on the first page of each 'Your Month At A Glance', under the title 'Highs and Lows'. The graph displays the lunar cycle and you will soon learn to understand how its movements have a bearing on your level of energy and your abilities.

Your Own Moon Sign

Discovering the position of the Moon at the time of your birth has always been notoriously difficult because tracking the complex zodiac positions of the Moon is not easy. This process has been reduced to three simple stages with Old Moore's unique Lunar Tables. A breakdown of the Moon's zodiac positions can be found from page 25 onwards, so that once you know what your Moon Sign is, you can see what part this plays in the overall build-up of your personal character.

If you follow the instructions on the next page you will soon be able to work out exactly what zodiac sign the Moon occupied on the day that you were born and you can then go on to compare the reading for this position with those of your Sun sign and your Ascendant. It is partly the comparison between these three important positions that goes towards making you the unique individual you are.

HOW TO DISCOVER YOUR MOON SIGN

This is a three-stage process. You may need a pen and a piece of paper but if you follow the instructions below the process should only take a minute or so.

STAGE 1 First of all you need to know the Moon Age at the time of your birth. If you look at Moon Table 1, on page 23, you will find all the years between 1914 and 2012 down the left side. Find the year of your birth and then trace across to the right to the month of your birth. Where the two intersect you will find a number. This is the date of the New Moon in the month that you were born. You now need to count forward the number of days between the New Moon and your own birthday. For example, if the New Moon in the month of your birth was shown as being the 6th and you were born on the 20th, your Moon Age Day would be 14. If the New Moon in the month of your birth came after your birthday, you need to count forward from the New Moon in the previous month. If you were born in a Leap Year, remember to count the 29th February. You can tell if your birth year was a Leap Year if the last two digits can be divided by four. Whatever the result, jot this number down so that you do not forget it.

STAGE 2 Take a look at Moon Table 2 on page 24. Down the left hand column look for the date of your birth. Now trace across to the month of your birth. Where the two meet you will find a letter. Copy this letter down alongside your Moon Age Day.

STAGE 3 Moon Table 3 on page 24 will supply you with the zodiac sign the Moon occupied on the day of your birth. Look for your Moon Age Day down the left hand column and then for the letter you found in Stage 2. Where the two converge you will find a zodiac sign and this is the sign occupied by the Moon on the day that you were born.

Your Zodiac Moon Sign Explained

You will find a profile of all zodiac Moon Signs on pages 25 to 28, showing in yet another way how astrology helps to make you into the individual that you are. In each daily entry of the Astral Diary you can find the zodiac position of the Moon for every day of the year. This also allows you to discover your lunar birthdays. Since the Moon passes through all the signs of the zodiac in about a month, you can expect something like twelve lunar birthdays each year. At these times you are likely to be emotionally steady and able to make the sort of decisions that have real, lasting value.

MOON TABLE 1

YEAR	FEB	MAR	APR	YEAR	FEB	MAR	APR	YEAR	FEB	MAR	APR
1914	24	26	24	1947	19	21	20	1980	15	16	15
1915	14	15	13	1948	9	11	9	1981	4	6	4
1916	3	5	3	1949	27	29	28	1982	23	24	23
1917	22	23	22	1950	16	18	17	1983	13	14	13
1918	11	12	11	1951	6	7	6	1984	1	2	1
1919	–	2/31	30	1952	25	25	24	1985	19	21	20
1920	19	20	18	1953	14	15	13	1986	9	10	9
1921	8	9	8	1954	3	5	3	1987	28	29	28
1922	26	28	27	1955	22	24	22	1988	17	18	16
1923	15	17	16	1956	11	12	11	1989	6	7	6
1924	5	5	4	1957	–	1/31	29	1990	25	26	25
1925	23	24	23	1958	18	20	19	1991	14	15	13
1926	12	14	12	1959	7	9	8	1992	3	4	3
1927	2	3	2	1960	26	27	26	1993	22	24	22
1928	19	21	20	1961	15	16	15	1994	10	12	11
1929	9	11	9	1962	5	6	5	1995	29	30	29
1930	28	30	28	1963	23	25	23	1996	18	19	18
1931	17	19	18	1964	13	14	12	1997	7	9	7
1932	6	7	6	1965	1	2	1	1998	26	27	26
1933	24	26	24	1966	19	21	20	1999	16	17	16
1934	14	15	13	1967	9	10	9	2000	5	6	4
1935	3	5	3	1968	28	29	28	2001	23	24	23
1936	22	23	21	1969	17	18	16	2002	12	13	12
1937	11	13	12	1970	6	7	6	2003	–	2	1
1938	–	2/31	30	1971	25	26	25	2004	20	21	19
1939	19	20	19	1972	14	15	13	2005	9	10	8
1940	8	9	7	1973	4	5	3	2006	28	29	27
1941	26	27	26	1974	22	24	22	2007	16	18	17
1942	15	16	15	1975	11	12	11	2008	6	7	6
1943	4	6	4	1976	29	30	29	2009	25	26	25
1944	24	24	22	1977	18	19	18	2010	14	15	14
1945	12	14	12	1978	7	9	7	2011	3	5	3
1946	2	3	2	1979	26	27	26	2012	22	22	21

TABLE 2

DAY	MAR	APR
1	F	J
2	G	J
3	G	J
4	G	J
5	G	J
6	G	J
7	G	J
8	G	J
9	G	J
10	G	J
11	G	K
12	H	K
13	H	K
14	H	K
15	H	K
16	H	K
17	H	K
18	H	K
19	H	K
20	H	K
21	H	L
22	I	L
23	I	L
24	I	L
25	I	L
26	I	L
27	I	L
28	I	L
29	I	L
30	I	L
31	I	–

TABLE 3

M/D	F	G	H	I	J	K	L
0	PI	PI	AR	AR	AR	TA	TA
1	PI	AR	AR	AR	TA	TA	TA
2	AR	AR	AR	TA	TA	TA	GE
3	AR	AR	TA	TA	TA	GE	GE
4	AR	TA	TA	GE	GE	GE	GE
5	TA	TA	GE	GE	GE	CA	CA
6	TA	GE	GE	GE	CA	CA	CA
7	GE	GE	GE	CA	CA	CA	LE
8	GE	GE	CA	CA	CA	LE	LE
9	CA	CA	CA	CA	LE	LE	VI
10	CA	CA	LE	LE	LE	VI	VI
11	CA	LE	LE	LE	VI	VI	VI
12	LE	LE	LE	VI	VI	VI	LI
13	LE	LE	VI	VI	VI	LI	LI
14	VI	VI	VI	LI	LI	LI	LI
15	VI	VI	LI	LI	LI	SC	SC
16	VI	LI	LI	LI	SC	SC	SC
17	LI	LI	LI	SC	SC	SC	SA
18	LI	LI	SC	SC	SC	SA	SA
19	LI	SC	SC	SC	SA	SA	SA
20	SC	SC	SA	SA	SA	CP	CP
21	SC	SA	SA	SA	CP	CP	CP
22	SC	SA	SA	CP	CP	CP	AQ
23	SA	SA	CP	CP	CP	AQ	AQ
24	SA	CP	CP	CP	AQ	AQ	AQ
25	CP	CP	AQ	AQ	AQ	PI	PI
26	CP	AQ	AQ	AQ	PI	PI	PI
27	AQ	AQ	AQ	PI	PI	PI	AR
28	AQ	AQ	PI	PI	PI	AR	AR
29	AQ	PI	PI	PI	AR	AR	AR

AR = Aries, TA = Taurus, GE = Gemini, CA = Cancer, LE = Leo, VI = Virgo, LI = Libra, SC = Scorpio, SA = Sagittarius, CP = Capricorn, AQ = Aquarius, PI = Pisces

MOON SIGNS

Moon in Aries

You have a strong imagination, courage, determination and a desire to do things in your own way and forge your own path through life.

Originality is a key attribute; you are seldom stuck for ideas although your mind is changeable and you could take the time to focus on individual tasks. Often quick-tempered, you take orders from few people and live life at a fast pace. Avoid health problems by taking regular time out for rest and relaxation.

Emotionally, it is important that you talk to those you are closest to and work out your true feelings. Once you discover that people are there to help, there is less necessity for you to do everything yourself.

Moon in Taurus

The Moon in Taurus gives you a courteous and friendly manner, which means you are likely to have many friends.

The good things in life mean a lot to you, as Taurus is an Earth sign that delights in experiences which please the senses. Hence you are probably a lover of good food and drink, which may in turn mean you need to keep an eye on the bathroom scales, especially as looking good is also important to you.

Emotionally you are fairly stable and you stick by your own standards. Taureans do not respond well to change. Intuition also plays an important part in your life.

Moon in Gemini

You have a warm-hearted character, sympathetic and eager to help others. At times reserved, you can also be articulate and chatty: this is part of the paradox of Gemini, which always brings duplicity to the nature. You are interested in current affairs, have a good intellect, and are good company and likely to have many friends. Most of your friends have a high opinion of you and would be ready to defend you should the need arise. However, this is usually unnecessary, as you are quite capable of defending yourself in any verbal confrontation.

Travel is important to your inquisitive mind and you find intellectual stimulus in mixing with people from different cultures. You also gain much from reading, writing and the arts but you do need plenty of rest and relaxation in order to avoid fatigue.

Moon in Cancer

The Moon in Cancer at the time of birth is a fortunate position as Cancer is the Moon's natural home. This means that the qualities of compassion and understanding given by the Moon are especially enhanced in your nature, and you are friendly and sociable and cope well with emotional pressures. You cherish home and family life, and happily do the domestic tasks. Your surroundings are important to you and you hate squalor and filth. You are likely to have a love of music and poetry.

Your basic character, although at times changeable like the Moon itself, depends on symmetry. You aim to make your surroundings comfortable and harmonious, for yourself and those close to you.

Moon in Leo

The best qualities of the Moon and Leo come together to make you warmhearted, fair, ambitious and self-confident. With good organisational abilities, you invariably rise to a position of responsibility in your chosen career. This is fortunate as you don't enjoy being an 'also-ran' and would rather be an important part of a small organisation than a menial in a large one.

You should be lucky in love, and happy, provided you put in the effort to make a comfortable home for yourself and those close to you. It is likely that you will have a love of pleasure, sport, music and literature. Life brings you many rewards, most of them as a direct result of your own efforts, although you may be luckier than average and ready to make the best of any situation.

Moon in Virgo

You are endowed with good mental abilities and a keen receptive memory, but you are never ostentatious or pretentious. Naturally quite reserved, you still have many friends, especially of the opposite sex. Marital relationships must be discussed carefully and worked at so that they remain harmonious, as personal attachments can be a problem if you do not give them your full attention.

Talented and persevering, you possess artistic qualities and are a good homemaker. Earning your honours through genuine merit, you work long and hard towards your objectives but show little pride in your achievements. Many short journeys will be undertaken in your life.

Moon in Libra

With the Moon in Libra you are naturally popular and make friends easily. People like you, probably more than you realise, you bring fun to a party and are a natural diplomat. For all its good points, Libra is not the most stable of astrological signs and, as a result, your emotions can be a little unstable too. Therefore, although the Moon in Libra is said to be good for love and marriage, your Sun sign and Rising sign will have an important effect on your emotional and loving qualities.

You must remember to relate to others in your decision-making. Co-operation is crucial because Libra represents the 'balance' of life that can only be achieved through harmonious relationships. Conformity is not easy for you because Libra, an Air sign, likes its independence.

Moon in Scorpio

Some people might call you pushy. In fact, all you really want to do is to live life to the full and protect yourself and your family from the pressures of life. Take care to avoid giving the impression of being sarcastic or impulsive and use your energies wisely and constructively.

You have great courage and you invariably achieve your goals by force of personality and sheer effort. You are fond of mystery and are good at predicting the outcome of situations and events. Travel experiences can be beneficial to you.

You may experience problems if you do not take time to examine your motives in a relationship, and also if you allow jealousy, always a feature of Scorpio, to cloud your judgement.

Moon in Sagittarius

The Moon in Sagittarius helps to make you a generous individual with humanitarian qualities and a kind heart. Restlessness may be intrinsic as your mind is seldom still. Perhaps because of this, you have a need for change that could lead you to several major moves during your adult life. You are not afraid to stand your ground when you know your judgement is right, you speak directly and have good intuition.

At work you are quick, efficient and versatile and so you make an ideal employee. You need work to be intellectually demanding and do not enjoy tedious routines.

In relationships, you anger quickly if faced with stupidity or deception, though you are just as quick to forgive and forget. Emotionally, there are times when your heart rules your head.

Moon in Capricorn

The Moon in Capricorn makes you popular and likely to come into the public eye in some way. The watery Moon is not entirely comfortable in the Earth sign of Capricorn and this may lead to some difficulties in the early years of life. An initial lack of creative ability and indecision must be overcome before the true qualities of patience and perseverance inherent in Capricorn can show through.

You have good administrative ability and are a capable worker, and if you are careful you can accumulate wealth. But you must be cautious and take professional advice in partnerships, as you are open to deception. You may be interested in social or welfare work, which suit your organisational skills and sympathy for others.

Moon in Aquarius

The Moon in Aquarius makes you an active and agreeable person with a friendly, easy-going nature. Sympathetic to the needs of others, you flourish in a laid-back atmosphere. You are broad-minded, fair and open to suggestion, although sometimes you have an unconventional quality which others can find hard to understand.

You are interested in the strange and curious, and in old articles and places. You enjoy trips to these places and gain much from them. Political, scientific and educational work interests you and you might choose a career in science or technology.

Money-wise, you make gains through innovation and concentration and Lunar Aquarians often tackle more than one job at a time. In love you are kind and honest.

Moon in Pisces

You have a kind, sympathetic nature, somewhat retiring at times, but you always take account of others' feelings and help when you can.

Personal relationships may be problematic, but as life goes on you can learn from your experiences and develop a better understanding of yourself and the world around you.

You have a fondness for travel, appreciate beauty and harmony and hate disorder and strife. You may be fond of literature and would make a good writer or speaker yourself. You have a creative imagination and may come across as an incurable romantic. You have strong intuition, maybe bordering on a mediumistic quality, which sets you apart from the mass. You may not be rich in cash terms, but your personal gifts are worth more than gold.

ARIES IN LOVE

Discover how compatible in love you are with people from the same and other signs of the zodiac. Five stars equals a match made in heaven!

Aries meets Aries

This could be an all-or-nothing pairing. Both parties are from a dominant sign, so someone will have to be flexible in order to maintain personal harmony. Both know what they want out of life, and may have trouble overcoming any obstacles a relationship creates. This is a good physical pairing, with a chemistry that few other matches enjoy to the same level. Attitude is everything, but at least there is a mutual admiration that makes gazing at your partner like looking in the mirror. Star rating: ****

Aries meets Taurus

This is a match that has been known to work very well. Aries brings dynamism and ambition, while Taurus has the patience to see things through logically. Such complementary views work equally well in a relationship or in the office. There is mutual respect, but sometimes a lack of total understanding. The romantic needs of each are quite different, but both are still fulfilled. They can live easily in domestic harmony which is very important but, interestingly, Aries may be the loser in battles of will. Star rating: ***

Aries meets Gemini

Don't expect peace and harmony with this combination, although what comes along instead might make up for any disagreements. Gemini has a very fertile imagination, while Aries has the tenacity to make reality from fantasy. Combined, they have a sizzling relationship. There are times when both parties could explode with indignation and something has to give. But even if there are clashes, making them up will always be most enjoyable! Mutual financial success is likely in this match. Star rating: ****

Aries meets Cancer

A potentially one-sided pairing, it often appears that the Cancerian is brow-beaten by the far more dominant Arian. So much depends on the patience of the Cancerian individual, because if good psychology is present – who knows? But beware, Aries, you may find your partner too passive, and constantly having to take the lead can be wearing – even for you. A prolonged trial period would be advantageous, as the match could easily go either way. When it does work, though, this relationship is usually contented. Star rating: ***

Aries meets Leo

Stand by for action and make sure the house is sound-proof. Leo is a lofty idealist and there is always likely to be friction when two Fire signs meet. To compensate, there is much mutual admiration, together with a desire to please. Where there are shared incentives, the prognosis is good but it's important not to let little irritations blow up. Both signs want to have their own way and this is a sure cause of trouble. There might not be much patience here, but there is plenty of action. Star rating: *****

Aries meets Virgo

Neither of these signs really understands the other, and that could easily lead to a clash. Virgo is so pedantic, which will drive Aries up the wall, while Aries always wants to be moving on to the next objective, before Virgo is even settled with the last one. It will take time for these two to get to know each other, but this is a great business matching. If a personal relationship is seen in these terms then the prognosis can be good, but on the whole, this is not an inspiring match. Star rating: ***

Aries meets Libra

These signs are zodiac opposites which means a make-or-break situation. The match will either be a great success or a dismal failure. Why? Well Aries finds it difficult to understand the flighty Air-sign tendencies of Libra, whilst the natural balance of Libra contradicts the unorthodox Arian methods. Any flexibility will come from Libra, which may mean that things work out for a while, but Libra only has so much patience and it may eventually run out. In the end, Aries may be just too bossy for an independent but sensitive sign like Libra. Star rating: **

Aries meets Scorpio

There can be great affection here, even if the two zodiac signs are so very different. The common link is the planet Mars, which plays a part in both these natures. Although Aries is, outwardly, the most dominant, Scorpio people are among the most powerful to be found anywhere. This quiet determination is respected by Aries. Aries will satisfy the passionate side of Scorpio, particularly with instruction from Scorpio. There are mysteries here which will add spice to life. The few arguments that do occur are likely to be awe-inspiring. Star rating: ****

Aries meets Sagittarius

This can be one of the most favourable matches of them all. Both Aries and Sagittarius are Fire signs, which often leads to clashes of will, but this pair find a mutual understanding. Sagittarius helps Aries to develop a better sense of humour, while Aries teaches the Archer about consistency on the road to success. Some patience is called for on both sides, but these people have a natural liking for each other. Add this to growing love and you have a long-lasting combination that is hard to beat. Star rating: *****

Aries meets Capricorn

Capricorn works conscientiously to achieve its objectives and so can be the perfect companion for Aries. The Ram knows how to achieve but not how to consolidate, so the two signs have a great deal to offer one another practically. There may not be fireworks and it's sometimes doubtful how well they know each other, but it may not matter. Aries is outwardly hot but inwardly cool, whilst Capricorn can appear low key but be a furnace underneath. Such a pairing can gradually find contentment, though both parties may wonder how this is so. Star rating: ****

Aries meets Aquarius

Aquarius is an Air sign, and Air and Fire often work well together, but perhaps not in the case of Aries and Aquarius. The average Aquarian lives in what the Ram sees as a fantasy world, so without a sufficiently good meeting of minds, compromise may be lacking. Of course, almost anything is possible, and the dominant side of Aries could be trained by the devil-may-care attitude of Aquarius. There are meeting points but they are difficult to establish. However, given sufficient time and an open mind on both sides, a degree of happiness is possible. Star rating: **

Aries meets Pisces

Still waters run deep, and they don't come much deeper than Pisces. Although these signs share the same quadrant of the zodiac, they have little in common. Pisces is a dreamer, a romantic idealist with steady and spiritual goals. Aries needs to be on the move, and has very different ideals. It's hard to see how a relationship could develop because the outlook on life is so different but, with patience, especially from Aries, there is a chance that things might work out. Pisces needs incentive, and Aries may be the sign to offer it. Star rating: **

VENUS:
THE PLANET OF LOVE

If you look up at the sky around sunset or sunrise you will often see Venus in close attendance to the Sun. It is arguably one of the most beautiful sights of all and there is little wonder that historically it became associated with the goddess of love. But although Venus does play an important part in the way you view love and in the way others see you romantically, this is only one of the spheres of influence that it enjoys in your overall character.

Venus has a part to play in the more cultured side of your life and has much to do with your appreciation of art, literature, music and general creativity. Even the way you look is responsive to the part of the zodiac that Venus occupied at the start of your life, though this fact is also down to your Sun sign and Ascending sign. If, at the time you were born, Venus occupied one of the more gregarious zodiac signs, you will be more likely to wear your heart on your sleeve, as well as to be more attracted to entertainment, social gatherings and good company. If on the other hand Venus occupied a quiet zodiac sign at the time of your birth, you would tend to be more retiring and less willing to shine in public situations.

It's good to know what part the planet Venus plays in your life, for it can have a great bearing on the way you appear to the rest of the world and since we all have to mix with others, you can learn to make the very best of what Venus has to offer you.

One of the great complications in the past has always been trying to establish exactly what zodiac position Venus enjoyed when you were born, because the planet is notoriously difficult to track. However, I have solved that problem by creating a table that is exclusive to your Sun sign, which you will find on the following page.

Establishing your Venus sign could not be easier. Just look up the year of your birth on the page opposite and you will see a sign of the zodiac. This was the sign that Venus occupied in the period covered by your sign in that year. If Venus occupied more than one sign during the period, this is indicated by the date on which the sign changed, and the name of the new sign. For instance, if you were born in 1950, Venus was in Aquarius until the 7th April, after which time it was in Pisces. If you were born before 7th April your Venus sign is Aquarius, if you were born on or after 7th April, your Venus sign is Pisces. Once you have established the position of Venus at the time of your birth, you can then look in the pages which follow to see how this has a bearing on your life as a whole.

1914 ARIES /14.4 TAURUS
1915 AQUARIUS / 1.4 PISCES
1916 TAURUS / 8.4 GEMINI
1917 PISCES / 28.3 ARIES
1918 AQUARIUS / 5.4 PISCES
1919 ARIES / 24.3 TAURUS
1920 PISCES / 14.4 ARIES
1921 TAURUS
1922 ARIES / 13.4 TAURUS
1923 AQUARIUS / 1.4 PISCES
1924 TAURUS / 6.4 GEMINI
1925 PISCES / 28.3 ARIES
1926 AQUARIUS / 6.4 PISCES
1927 ARIES / 24.3 TAURUS
1928 PISCES / 13.4 ARIES
1929 TAURUS / 20.4 ARIES
1930 ARIES / 13.4 TAURUS
1931 AQUARIUS / 31.3 PISCES
1932 TAURUS / 6.4 GEMINI
1933 PISCES / 27.3 ARIES
1934 AQUARIUS / 6.4 PISCES
1935 ARIES / 23.3 TAURUS
1936 PISCES / 13.4 ARIES
1937 TAURUS / 14.4 ARIES
1938 ARIES / 12.4 TAURUS
1939 AQUARIUS / 31.3 PISCES
1940 TAURUS / 5.4 GEMINI
1941 PISCES / 26.3 ARIES /
    20.4 TAURUS
1942 AQUARIUS / 7.4 PISCES
1943 ARIES / 23.3 TAURUS
1944 PISCES / 12.4 ARIES
1945 TAURUS / 8.4 ARIES
1946 ARIES / 12.4 TAURUS
1947 AQUARIUS / 30.3 PISCES
1948 TAURUS / 5.4 GEMINI
1949 PISCES / 25.3 ARIES /
    20.4 TAURUS
1950 AQUARIUS / 7.4 PISCES
1951 ARIES / 22.3 TAURUS
1952 PISCES / 12.4 ARIES
1953 TAURUS / 1.4 ARIES
1954 ARIES / 11.4 TAURUS
1955 AQUARIUS / 30.3 PISCES
1956 TAURUS / 4.4 GEMINI
1957 PISCES / 25.3 ARIES /
    19.4 TAURUS
1958 AQUARIUS / 8.4 PISCES
1959 ARIES / 22.3 TAURUS
1960 PISCES / 11.4 ARIES
1961 ARIES
1962 ARIES / 11.4 TAURUS
1963 AQUARIUS / 29.3 PISCES
1964 TAURUS / 4.4 GEMINI

1965 PISCES / 24.3 ARIES /
    19.4 TAURUS
1966 AQUARIUS / 8.4 PISCES
1967 TAURUS / 20.4 GEMINI
1968 PISCES / 10.4 ARIES
1969 ARIES
1970 ARIES / 10.4 TAURUS
1971 AQUARIUS / 29.3 PISCES
1972 TAURUS / 3.4 GEMINI
1973 PISCES / 24.3 ARIES /
    18.4 TAURUS
1974 AQUARIUS / 8.4 PISCES
1975 TAURUS / 19.4 GEMINI
1976 PISCES / 10.4 ARIES
1977 ARIES
1978 ARIES / 10.4 TAURUS
1979 AQUARIUS / 28.3 PISCES
1980 TAURUS / 3.4 GEMINI
1981 PISCES / 23.3 ARIES /
    18.4 TAURUS
1982 AQUARIUS / 9.4 PISCES
1983 TAURUS / 19.4 GEMINI
1984 PISCES / 9.4 ARIES
1985 ARIES
1986 ARIES / 9.4 TAURUS
1987 AQUARIUS / 28.3 PISCES
1988 TAURUS / 2.4 GEMINI
1989 PISCES / 23.3 ARIES /
    17.4 TAURUS
1990 AQUARIUS / 9.4 PISCES
1991 TAURUS / 18.4 GEMINI
1992 PISCES / 9.4 ARIES
1993 ARIES
1994 ARIES / 9.4 TAURUS
1995 AQUARIUS / 27.3 PISCES
1996 TAURUS / 2.4 GEMINI
1997 PISCES / 22.3 ARIES /
    17.4 TAURUS
1998 AQUARIUS / 9.4 PISCES
1999 TAURUS / 18.4 GEMINI
2000 PISCES / 9.4 ARIES
2001 ARIES
2002 ARIES / 7.4 TAURUS
2003 AQUARIUS / 27.3 PISCES
2004 TAURUS / 1.4 GEMINI
2005 PISCES/22.3 ARIES
2006 AQUARIUS / 7.4 PISCES
2007 TAURUS / 16.4 GEMINI
2008 PISCES / 9.4 ARIES
2009 ARIES
2010 ARIES / 7.4 TAURUS
2011 AQUARIUS / 27.3 PISCES
2012 TAURUS / 1.4 GEMINI

VENUS THROUGH THE ZODIAC SIGNS

Venus in Aries

Amongst other things, the position of Venus in Aries indicates a fondness for travel, music and all creative pursuits. Your nature tends to be affectionate and you would try not to create confusion or difficulty for others if it could be avoided. Many people with this planetary position have a great love of the theatre, and mental stimulation is of the greatest importance. Early romantic attachments are common with Venus in Aries, so it is very important to establish a genuine sense of romantic continuity. Early marriage is not recommended, especially if it is based on sympathy. You may give your heart a little too readily on occasions.

Venus in Taurus

You are capable of very deep feelings and your emotions tend to last for a very long time. This makes you a trusting partner and lover, whose constancy is second to none. In life you are precise and careful and always try to do things the right way. Although this means an ordered life, which you are comfortable with, it can also lead you to be rather too fussy for your own good. Despite your pleasant nature, you are very fixed in your opinions and quite able to speak your mind. Others are attracted to you and historical astrologers always quoted this position of Venus as being very fortunate in terms of marriage. However, if you find yourself involved in a failed relationship, it could take you a long time to trust again.

Venus in Gemini

As with all associations related to Gemini, you tend to be quite versatile, anxious for change and intelligent in your dealings with the world at large. You may gain money from more than one source but you are equally good at spending it. There is an inference here that you are a good communicator, via either the written or the spoken word, and you love to be in the company of interesting people. Always on the look-out for culture, you may also be very fond of music, and love to indulge the curious and cultured side of your nature. In romance you tend to have more than one relationship and could find yourself associated with someone who has previously been a friend or even a distant relative.

Venus in Cancer

You often stay close to home because you are very fond of family and enjoy many of your most treasured moments when you are with those you love. Being naturally sympathetic, you will always do anything you can to support those around you, even people you hardly know at all. This charitable side of your nature is your most noticeable trait and is one of the reasons why others are naturally so fond of you. Being receptive and in some cases even psychic, you can see through to the soul of most of those with whom you come into contact. You may not commence too many romantic attachments but when you do give your heart, it tends to be unconditionally.

Venus in Leo

It must become quickly obvious to almost anyone you meet that you are kind, sympathetic and yet determined enough to stand up for anyone or anything that is truly important to you. Bright and sunny, you warm the world with your natural enthusiasm and would rarely do anything to hurt those around you, or at least not intentionally. In romance you are ardent and sincere, though some may find your style just a little overpowering. Gains come through your contacts with other people and this could be especially true with regard to romance, for love and money often come hand in hand for those who were born with Venus in Leo. People claim to understand you, though you are more complex than you seem.

Venus in Virgo

Your nature could well be fairly quiet no matter what your Sun sign might be, though this fact often manifests itself as an inner peace and would not prevent you from being basically sociable. Some delays and even the odd disappointment in love cannot be ruled out with this planetary position, though it's a fact that you will usually find the happiness you look for in the end. Catapulting yourself into romantic entanglements that you know to be rather ill-advised is not sensible, and it would be better to wait before you committed yourself exclusively to any one person. It is the essence of your nature to serve the world at large and through doing so it is possible that you will attract money at some stage in your life.

Venus in Libra

Venus is very comfortable in Libra and bestows upon those people who have this planetary position a particular sort of kindness that is easy to recognise. This is a very good position for all sorts of friendships and also for romantic attachments that usually bring much joy into your life. Few individuals with Venus in Libra would avoid marriage and since you are capable of great depths of love, it is likely that you will find a contented personal life. You like to mix with people of integrity and intelligence but don't take kindly to scruffy surroundings or work that means getting your hands too dirty. Careful speculation, good business dealings and money through marriage all seem fairly likely.

Venus in Scorpio

You are quite open and tend to spend money quite freely, even on those occasions when you don't have very much. Although your intentions are always good, there are times when you get yourself in to the odd scrape and this can be particularly true when it comes to romance, which you may come to late or from a rather unexpected direction. Certainly you have the power to be happy and to make others contented on the way, but you find the odd stumbling block on your journey through life and it could seem that you have to work harder than those around you. As a result of this, you gain a much deeper understanding of the true value of personal happiness than many people ever do, and are likely to achieve true contentment in the end.

Venus in Sagittarius

You are lighthearted, cheerful and always able to see the funny side of any situation. These facts enhance your popularity, which is especially high with members of the opposite sex. You should never have to look too far to find romantic interest in your life, though it is just possible that you might be too willing to commit yourself before you are certain that the person in question is right for you. Part of the problem here extends to other areas of life too. The fact is that you like variety in everything and so can tire of situations that fail to offer it. All the same, if you choose wisely and learn to understand your restless side, then great happiness can be yours.

Venus in Capricorn

The most notable trait that comes from Venus in this position is that it makes you trustworthy and able to take on all sorts of responsibilities in life. People are instinctively fond of you and love you all the more because you are always ready to help those who are in any form of need. Social and business popularity can be yours and there is a magnetic quality to your nature that is particularly attractive in a romantic sense. Anyone who wants a partner for a lover, a spouse and a good friend too would almost certainly look in your direction. Constancy is the hallmark of your nature and unfaithfulness would go right against the grain. You might sometimes be a little too trusting.

Venus in Aquarius

This location of Venus offers a fondness for travel and a desire to try out something new at every possible opportunity. You are extremely easy to get along with and tend to have many friends from varied backgrounds, classes and inclinations. You like to live a distinct sort of life and gain a great deal from moving about, both in a career sense and with regard to your home. It is not out of the question that you could form a romantic attachment to someone who comes from far away or be attracted to a person of a distinctly artistic and original nature. What you cannot stand is jealousy, for you have friends of both sexes and would want to keep things that way.

Venus in Pisces

The first thing people tend to notice about you is your wonderful, warm smile. Being very charitable by nature you will do anything to help others, even if you don't know them well. Much of your life may be spent sorting out situations for other people, but it is very important to feel that you are living for yourself too. In the main, you remain cheerful, and tend to be quite attractive to members of the opposite sex. Where romantic attachments are concerned, you could be drawn to people who are significantly older or younger than yourself or to someone with a unique career or point of view. It might be best for you to avoid marrying whilst you are still very young.

THE ASTRAL DIARY
HOW THE DIAGRAMS WORK

Through the picture diagrams in the Astral Diary I want to help you to plot your year. With them you can see where the positive and negative aspects will be found in each month. To make the most of them, all you have to do is remember where and when!

Let me show you how they work ...

THE MONTH AT A GLANCE

Just as there are twelve separate zodiac signs, so astrologers believe that each sign has twelve separate aspects to life. Each of the twelve segments relates to a different personal aspect. I list them all every month so that their meanings are always clear.

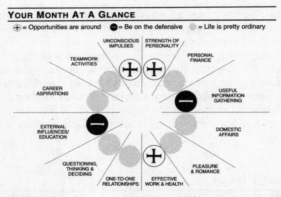

I have designed this chart to show you how and when these twelve different aspects are being influenced throughout the year. When there is a shaded circle, nothing out of the ordinary is to be expected. However, when a circle turns white with a plus sign, the influence is positive. Where the circle is black with a minus sign, it is a negative.

YOUR ENERGY RHYTHM CHART

On the opposite page is a picture diagram in which I link your zodiac group to the rhythm of the Moon. In doing this I have calculated when you will be gaining strength from its influence and equally when you may be weakened by it.

If you think of yourself as being like the tides of the ocean then you may understand how your own energies must also rise and fall. And if you understand how it works and when it is working, then you can better organise your activities to achieve more and get things done more easily.

YOUR ENERGY RHYTHM CHART

At your best on 20th–21st

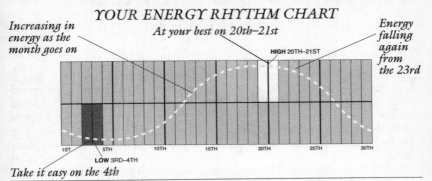

Increasing in energy as the month goes on

Energy falling again from the 23rd

HIGH 20TH–21ST

1ST 5TH 10TH 15TH 20TH 25TH 30TH

LOW 3RD–4TH

Take it easy on the 4th

MOVING PICTURE SCREEN

Love, money, career and vitality measured every week

The diagram at the end of each week is designed to be informative and fun. The arrows move up and down the scale to give you an idea of the strength of your opportunities in each area. If LOVE stands at plus 4, then get out and put yourself about because things are going your way in romance! The further down the arrow goes, the weaker the opportunities. Do note that the diagram is an overall view of your astrological aspects and therefore reflects a trend which may not concur with every day in that cycle.

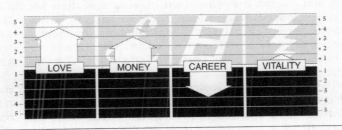

| LOVE | MONEY | CAREER | VITALITY |

AND FINALLY:

am ....

pm ....

The two lines that are left blank in each daily entry of the Astral Diary are for your own personal use. You may find them ideal for keeping a check on birthdays or appointments, though it could also be an idea to make notes from the astrological trends and diagrams a few weeks in advance. Some of the lines are marked with a key, which indicates the working of astrological cycles in your life. Look out for them each week as they are the best days to take action or make decisions. The daily text tells you which area of your life to focus on.

☿ = Mercury is retrograde on that day.

ARIES: YOUR YEAR IN BRIEF

You should find the start of the year to be generally positive, and it begins with a punch. Later in January you may get slightly depressed by the winter weather but if you keep yourself active you should soon find the time passing usefully and successfully. Routines can be a chore late in the month, but keep active and show what an enterprising side you have to your nature. January and February are both potentially fortunate months.

March and April could bring their own small problems, but in the end you should discover that with patience and perseverance you can overcome obstacles and push through to your chosen destination. March especially is good for romance, whilst April is more materialistic in nature and depends a great deal on your own ingenuity, which is right on the ball throughout most of the month.

With the start of the summer, May and June encourage you to be in a very positive frame of mind, more inclined to travel and extremely sociable in your attitude. There are gains to be made as a result of romance and a new start possible at work, even if you are not actually pursuing such a thing. The attitude of friends in June could be somewhat odd and almost anyone can cause you little problems, though not for long at a time.

July and August have their own benefits, and these should become more or less immediately obvious. There are gains to be made as a result of past and present efforts, as well as through the involvement in your life of new people or those you haven't seen for quite some time. Throughout most of this period you will be active and anxious to score a number of successes.

As the autumn arrives, September and October should offer you scope to achieve more of your objectives and you will also be right on the ball when it comes to love and romance. New relationships can commence now and there is a strong sense of purpose in almost everything you do. Don't be put out by the fact that colleagues are behaving strangely. Accept their point of view, no matter how odd it might seem to be.

At the end of the year, November and December can prove to be a very memorable time and a period during which you show yourself to be fully conversant with everything that is going on around you. There are financial gains to be made in November, but money to be spent in December, so it will probably all balance out! Finish the year in the most optimistic frame of mind you can manage. Your creative potential is excellent as the year draws to a close.

January 2012

YOUR MONTH AT A GLANCE

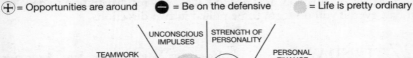

⊕ = Opportunities are around ⊖ = Be on the defensive ● = Life is pretty ordinary

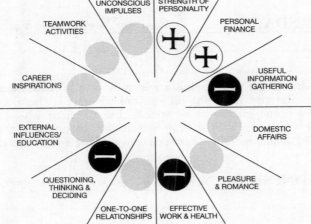

UNCONSCIOUS IMPULSES

STRENGTH OF PERSONALITY

TEAMWORK ACTIVITIES

PERSONAL FINANCE

CAREER INSPIRATIONS

USEFUL INFORMATION GATHERING

EXTERNAL INFLUENCES/ EDUCATION

DOMESTIC AFFAIRS

QUESTIONING, THINKING & DECIDING

PLEASURE & ROMANCE

ONE-TO-ONE RELATIONSHIPS

EFFECTIVE WORK & HEALTH

JANUARY HIGHS AND LOWS

Here I show you how the rhythms of the Moon will affect you this month. Like the tide, your energies and abilities will rise and fall with its pattern. When it is above the centre line, go for it, when it is below, you should be resting.

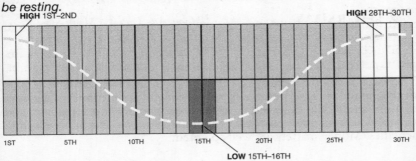

HIGH 1ST–2ND

HIGH 28TH–30TH

LOW 15TH–16TH

1ST 5TH 10TH 15TH 20TH 25TH 30TH

26 MONDAY
Moon Age Day 1   Moon Sign Capricorn

am ....

pm...

Boxing Day could offer time for reflection, but probably not much. Involvement with your family may well be rewarding, though it does mean your mind will be diverted from the more practical considerations that usually occupy you. You needn't allow any real frustration to develop today, even if you do seem to be pulled in two directions.

27 TUESDAY
Moon Age Day 2   Moon Sign Aquarius

am ....

pm...

Trends indicate that your friends are literally your greatest asset now, so make sure that you are doing all you can to support them. It's worth taking some time out to be of specific use to those who have been important to you for a long time, whilst also giving some thought to entertaining family members between now and the end of the year.

28 WEDNESDAY
Moon Age Day 3   Moon Sign Aquarius

am ....

pm...

You have a clear and analytical mind, and if you make full use of it now you shouldn't have any difficulty sorting out puzzles that really stump others. While friends and family members are scratching their heads, you have solved the problem and will be moving onto the next one. Your dexterity should be the talk of any party today.

29 THURSDAY
Moon Age Day 4   Moon Sign Pisces

am ....

pm...

The focus is still on friends, as well as on your involvement with groups or organisations. This is especially the case if you are involved in activities that are specifically designed to help those who are less fortunate, and you may also be quite physically committed today – maybe in sporting activities. Money matters are well accented.

30 FRIDAY
Moon Age Day 5   Moon Sign Pisces

am ....

pm ....

It is quite possible that the further you roam today, the better you are likely to feel. One option is to seek the wide blue yonder and if possible take a long walk. The wind should blow away any holiday cobwebs and you will end up feeling better about yourself and life generally. Plan today for any celebrations that are taking place tomorrow.

31 SATURDAY
Moon Age Day 6   Moon Sign Pisces

am ....

pm ....

You have scope to end the year on a generally high note, because although it doesn't show early in the day, the lunar high will be with you before the cries of 'Happy New Year' begin. This is all you need to make yourself the life and soul of the party, and that could well include doing something quite silly and very amusing!

1 SUNDAY
Moon Age Day 7   Moon Sign Aries

am ....

pm ....

What a great way this is to start the year! With the lunar high present you have everything you need to be on top form. It's time to put your sharp mind to work thinking up new strategies to make this year go with a zing. Attitude is really important when you turn your mind to matters that have been irritating you.

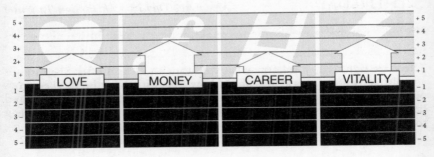

2 MONDAY
Moon Age Day 8   Moon Sign Aries

am ....

pm ....

Things are still looking favourable, and if you are back at work today you should be able to push forward positively into new avenues. You have potential to come up with some extremely ingenious strategies, and also to enlist the support of people who recognise how capable you are. Colleagues and bosses alike could be lining up to support you.

3 TUESDAY
Moon Age Day 9   Moon Sign Taurus

am ....

pm ....

With Mars in its present position this is a good day for getting things done. Don't try to rush your fences, even if you sense that speed is of the essence. The more you check and double-check things, the better you can get life going for you. This is also a very good time for starting a new romantic adventure or for pepping up an existing one.

4 WEDNESDAY
Moon Age Day 10   Moon Sign Taurus

am ....

pm ....

During this time there are gains to be made from seeking out new friendships and making the most of what those around you have to offer. Aries can now afford to be less selfish than can sometimes be the case, and you should be quite happy to put yourself out to offer some timely assistance to people who really need it.

5 THURSDAY
Moon Age Day 11   Moon Sign Taurus

am ....

pm ....

There are signs that you know what you want and – as is often the case – you also have a very good idea about how to get it. Don't be too keen to put yourself forward for jobs you don't really understand. It would be far better at the moment to do a little homework. That way you will be able to show just how efficient and competent you are.

6 FRIDAY
Moon Age Day 12   Moon Sign Gemini

am ....

pm...

Around now you are encouraged to look at the more philosophical side of life, and might be quite happy to sit and scratch your head for a while, instead of pitching in and getting yourself in a muddle. Working out how and why things work in the way they do could prove to be quite entertaining, and is a good way to pass some time now.

7 SATURDAY
Moon Age Day 13   Moon Sign Gemini

am ....

pm...

Even if you are presently keen to satisfy your own needs and wants in life, it's possible that people close to you will still be expecting a great deal from you. It won't always be easy to satisfy everyone's demands, and there might be occasions today when it would be much better to simply admit that you don't have all the answers.

8 SUNDAY
Moon Age Day 14   Moon Sign Cancer

am ....

pm...

With the Moon in its present position you should now be much more aware of your needs in terms of personal security. For this reason you might decide to save money rather than to spend it rashly. Getting family finances in order may be another issue you are able to address early in the year. But will everyone appreciate your interference?

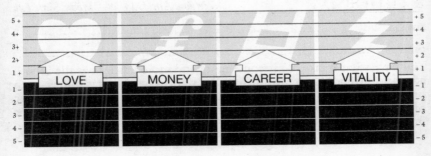

9 MONDAY
Moon Age Day 15   Moon Sign Cancer

am ....

pm..

Now you need to make the most of whatever is happening on the social front. There is much to be said for creating a good impression in the eyes of people who are definitely in a position to help you, and you need to call on the positive resources of colleagues and friends alike. It's simply a question of persuading them to return favours.

10 TUESDAY
Moon Age Day 16   Moon Sign Cancer

am ....

pm..

Creating situations that can be fun for everyone concerned should be a natural part of life now. This is the most attractive side of Aries because your imagination is strong and you can see through others as if they were made of glass. Look out for more vulnerable people today, as well as animals that may need your protection more than usual.

11 WEDNESDAY
Moon Age Day 17   Moon Sign Leo

am ....

pm..

A day to use your energy to plan work moves and to help other people to get ahead in their chosen career. This would be an ideal time to offer advice to younger people or to those who are making a genuine fresh start in life. Aries sometimes champions the underdog, and that is exactly what suits the present astrological scene.

12 THURSDAY
Moon Age Day 18   Moon Sign Leo

am ....

pm..

You have what it takes to become more and more efficient as the month advances. Trends assist you to find the right way of doing things, even on those occasions when others doubt your abilities. Have the courage of your convictions and argue for a course of action that you know to be both wise and potentially profitable.

13 FRIDAY
Moon Age Day 19   Moon Sign Virgo

am ....

pm...

Even if things get off to a fairly slow start today, you can still make progress if you don't try to push too hard before the time is right. The lunar low is approaching, and that isn't an ideal time for you to try to accomplish too much. That is why it is important to choose your moves carefully and to do a few things properly.

14 SATURDAY
Moon Age Day 20   Moon Sign Virgo

am ....

pm...

The best advice for today is simply to keep up the good work. It's amazing just how much you can achieve by following on from someone who is clearly in the know. Don't assume that you have all the answers yourself, especially in matters that are new to you. There is no shame in asking others for guidance.

15 SUNDAY
Moon Age Day 21   Moon Sign Libra

am ....

pm...

Be prepared to slow things down today. You have arrived at that time when the Moon occupies your opposite zodiac sign of Libra, bringing a period known as the lunar low. This can be a time of regeneration, though it is not the best period for embarking on anything new or particularly exciting. You need to be quite circumspect today.

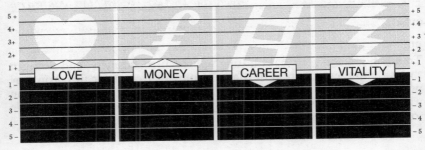

16 MONDAY   *Moon Age Day 22   Moon Sign Libra*

am ....

pm...

If you find you are somewhat oversensitive today, you need to consider whether this is influenced by the present position of the Moon. You would be wise not to react too harshly to things, or to snap at people even if they are saying things you don't care for. Watch and wait. It shouldn't be long before you can get yourself right back on form.

17 TUESDAY   *Moon Age Day 23   Moon Sign Scorpio*

am ....

pm...

One-to-one relationships may seem to have a few drawbacks at the moment, thanks to the present position of Venus in your solar twelfth house. You can be too thoughtful for your own good and may be inclined to see personal problems where none really exist. It won't be long before Venus moves on, but for now, avoid reacting too harshly.

18 WEDNESDAY   *Moon Age Day 24   Moon Sign Scorpio*

am ....

pm...

If things go wrong today, think carefully before you blame other people. In the main you have everything you need to keep progressing in life, even if it doesn't look like that on occasions. The lunar low is now well out of the way, so you do have what it takes to start moving forward again. There's nothing wrong with taking things slowly at first.

19 THURSDAY   *Moon Age Day 25   Moon Sign Sagittarius*

am ....

pm...

Trends highlight your hard-hitting approach to business, and you can thank the present position of Mars in your solar chart for this. You may not take kindly to interference, and it is clear that you know what you want, even in the face of others disagreeing. Remember that it's possible to get your own way without ruffling too many feathers.

20 FRIDAY
Moon Age Day 26   Moon Sign Sagittarius

am...

pm...

Travel and getting about generally could prove to be interesting, and you are unlikely to get everything you really want from life at the moment if you choose to stay in the same place all the time. Whether or not you can persuade other people to go with you is another matter. Be prepared to deal with a few stick-in-the-mud types now.

21 SATURDAY
Moon Age Day 27   Moon Sign Capricorn

am...

pm...

In professional developments your insights are now second to none. Even if you can't actually make any solid moves at the weekend, you should certainly be able to look ahead and plan carefully. Standing on the edge of things is not a place you like to be, and in most sporting or personal activities you can afford to really get involved today.

22 SUNDAY
Moon Age Day 28   Moon Sign Capricorn

am...

pm...

There is something of a search for inner security going on within you at this time, and this could leave you a little more vulnerable to supposed emotional attacks than would normally be the case. You need to ask whether in fact you are making mountains out of molehills. Why not get on with something practical and leave the psychology to others for now?

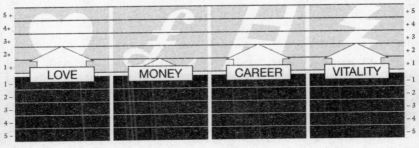

23 MONDAY
Moon Age Day 0   Moon Sign Capricorn

am ....

pm ....

Do beware of alienating certain people at this time by reacting harshly to their ideas or by being dismissive. Aries can be something of a bully on occasions, even though this is the last thing you actually want to be. Your best approach is to listen carefully to those around you. If you have to disagree, do so after making certain of your own ground.

24 TUESDAY
Moon Age Day 1   Moon Sign Aquarius

am ....

pm ....

Self-confidence is the name of the game, and as the month advances you should have better and better ideas about the way you want things to be. Not everyone is quite as progressive as you are, which is why it might sometimes feel as though you are towing people along behind you. Aries is now on top form, but should still take life steadily.

25 WEDNESDAY
Moon Age Day 2   Moon Sign Aquarius

am ....

pm ....

At this time practical matters might not exactly be your best area of life. If things go wrong, you could well decide to call upon some practical assistance. Just appreciate that, as clever as you are, you can't do everything. Experts are needed, and the skill is in finding just the right people to sort certain things out for you.

26 THURSDAY
Moon Age Day 3   Moon Sign Pisces

am ....

pm ....

Now you are encouraged to do some deep thinking, and with Venus still in your solar twelfth house it is towards relationships of one sort or another that your mind should be ready to turn. Standing up for yourself at work is all very well, but there could be occasions when you are defending yourself long before you have been attacked.

27 FRIDAY
Moon Age Day 4   Moon Sign Pisces

am ....

pm...

Beware of beginning anything new until you have finished a current project. There is usually no difficulty in Aries dealing with half a dozen different jobs at the same time, but for the moment you need to be quite discriminating. A great triumph is within your reach, but it may need every ounce of your concentration to get things right.

28 SATURDAY
Moon Age Day 5   Moon Sign Aries

am ....

pm...

Your originality and inventiveness are very definitely to the fore today, as the Moon races back into your own zodiac sign and assists you to get right back into the frame. You can persuade almost anyone to lend a hand, particularly if they recognise that you are going places. Be adventurous and show yourself to the world as you truly are.

29 SUNDAY
Moon Age Day 6   Moon Sign Aries

am ....

pm...

Following up on your naturally creative instincts is a positive thing to do while the Moon stays in your sign. Be certain to let people know what you want. You have what it takes to get those around to actively follow you, wherever you decide to go. And what a great day this can be as far as personal attachments are concerned.

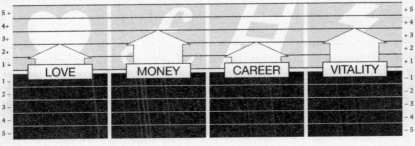

30 MONDAY
Moon Age Day 7   Moon Sign Aries

am ....

pm...

For the third day in a row the Moon is with you in the sign of Aries, and that allows you to start the new week in a very positive frame of mind. With everything to play for you need to express yourself positively at every turn, and you shouldn't shy away from anything, even if it is an issue that has given you problems before.

31 TUESDAY
Moon Age Day 8   Moon Sign Taurus

am ....

pm...

Venus still has not moved on, so it's worth showing patience to those you care about, even if you feel that some of them are behaving in a less than wise way. Look to people's strengths, but also recognise their weaknesses, and remember that you have a few of your own! The right attitude is certainly important at this time.

1 WEDNESDAY
Moon Age Day 9   Moon Sign Taurus

am ....

pm...

The first day of a new month should find you in fine spirits and looking around yourself for the first signs of spring to be emerging. When it comes to making money you have everything you need to be on top form, and should be able to express yourself well, no matter what company you are in. Love shines brightly in your heart around this time.

2 THURSDAY
Moon Age Day 10   Moon Sign Gemini

am ....

pm...

Concern for the needs and wants of those close to you is indicated now, and this encourages you to be especially sympathetic, both today and for several more days to come. There is a lot taking place in your solar twelfth house at this time, which assists you to think more deeply. The emphasis is on well-considered actions.

3 FRIDAY
Moon Age Day 11   Moon Sign Gemini

am ....

pm ....

Your main focus for the moment should be on friendship and team activities. Although Aries usually wants to be out in front and leading the pack, there are times when it is better for you to watch and to see how others behave. Keeping an eye open can help you in many ways right now, not least in terms of your love life.

4 SATURDAY
Moon Age Day 12   Moon Sign Gemini

am ....

pm ....

New meetings could well have a part to play in your life this weekend. This isn't the time to lock yourself away at home, no matter what the weather is doing. It would be better by far to stay out and about as much as you can. Friends might have some novel ideas for how to spend the evening, and you could do worse than to get yourself involved.

5 SUNDAY
Moon Age Day 13   Moon Sign Cancer

am ....

pm ....

Get ready for a period of fairly hard work to come. Mars remains in a potent position for you, and although Sunday is traditionally a day of rest, this isn't necessarily the case as far as you are concerned. Even if you are not actually doing anything, your mind should be working overtime, and it is clear that you have your planning head on.

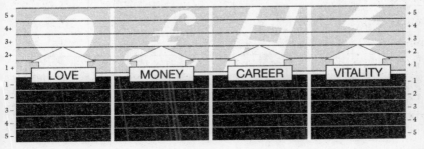

February

2012

YOUR MONTH AT A GLANCE

⊕ = Opportunities are around ⊖ = Be on the defensive ⬤ = Life is pretty ordinary

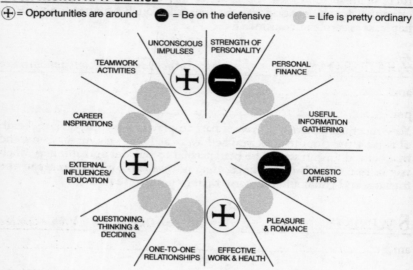

- UNCONSCIOUS IMPULSES ⊕
- STRENGTH OF PERSONALITY ⊖
- TEAMWORK ACTIVITIES
- PERSONAL FINANCE
- CAREER INSPIRATIONS
- USEFUL INFORMATION GATHERING
- EXTERNAL INFLUENCES/ EDUCATION ⊕
- DOMESTIC AFFAIRS ⊖
- QUESTIONING, THINKING & DECIDING
- PLEASURE & ROMANCE
- ONE-TO-ONE RELATIONSHIPS
- EFFECTIVE WORK & HEALTH ⊕

FEBRUARY HIGHS AND LOWS

Here I show you how the rhythms of the Moon will affect you this month. Like the tide, your energies and abilities will rise and fall with its pattern. When it is above the centre line, go for it, when it is below, you should be resting.

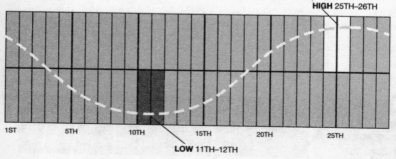

HIGH 25TH–26TH

1ST 5TH 10TH 15TH 20TH 25TH

LOW 11TH–12TH

6 MONDAY

Moon Age Day 14   Moon Sign Cancer

am ....

pm ....

The Moon is in your solar fourth house today and that is likely to inspire strong feelings associated with home and family. Even if you are still busy, there is much to be said for spending more time thinking about those closest to you and working out what you can do to keep everyone as happy as proves to be possible.

7 TUESDAY

Moon Age Day 15   Moon Sign Leo

am ....

pm ....

You have what it takes to manipulate events right now, using a combination of common sense and your magnetic personality. However, bear in mind that you can't control everything, and there may be times right now when you will have to rely on the good offices of friends or colleagues. Don't be frightened to ask if you need a favour.

8 WEDNESDAY

Moon Age Day 16   Moon Sign Leo

am ....

pm ....

Make the most of a potentially beneficial time as far as group activities are concerned. You have the natural ability to make yourself the leader in many situations, and this could certainly be the case at this time. The Sun in its present position in your solar chart gives you plenty of opportunity to get your personal affairs well in order.

9 THURSDAY

Moon Age Day 17   Moon Sign Virgo

am ....

pm ....

This is a time to be cautious and to study the details of any business deal very carefully. If you have to sign a document, it's worth making sure you look at the small print first, and avoid being conned into thinking that the grass really is all that green on the other side of the fence. Sometimes you are best sticking to what you know.

10 FRIDAY

Moon Age Day 18   Moon Sign Virgo

am ....

pm...

Present relationships could well become closer and closer as February moves on. This would also be an ideal time to try and heal any breaches that have been around for a while, perhaps within the family. The focus is firmly on the giving and understanding side of your nature now. Your creative potential can be used for making changes at home.

11 SATURDAY

Moon Age Day 19   Moon Sign Libra

am ....

pm...

Energy levels could well be flagging now as the lunar low comes along. It can take the wind out of your sails, and this is not the best time of the month for putting your most ambitious plans into action. It pays to watch and wait for a couple of days, while monitoring the way others are behaving and how they might be thinking.

12 SUNDAY

Moon Age Day 20   Moon Sign Libra

am ....

pm...

Does it seem that things are generally limited today? In reality you are in a good position to make progress, but not at this exact moment. This should be a time of consolidation and a period during which you are sharpening your weapons for later. Concentrate on one thing at once and make sure everything is done properly.

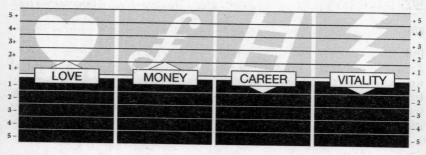

13 MONDAY
Moon Age Day 21   Moon Sign Scorpio

am ....

pm ....

At last Venus has moved on in your chart and it now stands in your solar first house. This can offer you a stimulus in your personal life, and the start of this week could well coincide with new romantic developments of one sort or another. If you show how charming you can be, there is no doubt that people will want to have you around.

14 TUESDAY
Moon Age Day 22   Moon Sign Scorpio

am ....

pm ....

A time for feeling particularly happy and relaxed when you are with your friends. This is an ideal interlude in which to expand your social life and to show the world at large just how outgoing and cheerful you actually are. You also need to capitalise on opportunities to prove that you are not quite as intense as people might have thought.

15 WEDNESDAY
Moon Age Day 23   Moon Sign Scorpio

am ....

pm ....

The emphasis on the sympathetic and considerate side of your nature continues, and you can use this to increase your general popularity. The position of little Mercury in your solar twelfth house encourages you to be more sacrificing and submissive than would usually be the case. This relates to your actions as well as your words.

16 THURSDAY
Moon Age Day 24   Moon Sign Sagittarius

am ....

pm ....

Your present frame of mind assists you to bring harmony to social functions, and even people who usually get on your nerves are less likely to do so at the moment. Be ready to offer help or support to anyone who wants something from you. This could be the happiest part of February in many ways.

17 FRIDAY
Moon Age Day 25   Moon Sign Sagittarius

am ....

pm ....

It's up to you to capitalise on new and promising possibilities at work, just ahead of the weekend. Today would be a good time to get something you want from someone who is higher up the career tree than you are. Confidence to do the right thing when in romantic situations is emphasised, and there is no doubting your present charm.

18 SATURDAY
Moon Age Day 26   Moon Sign Capricorn

am ....

pm ....

You would be wise to be just a little careful today and avoid getting involved in unnecessary conflicts. These may not be your own fault, particularly if certain individuals are not behaving in a very rational way. The best way forward is to get to the bottom of situations and find out what is really going on, even if you have to do some digging.

19 SUNDAY
Moon Age Day 27   Moon Sign Capricorn

am ....

pm ....

You can find solace and peace in a little meditation today. It's worth getting right away from any sort of conflict that is taking place in your vicinity and where possible allowing others to make the running for now. Meanwhile, there's nothing wrong with being happiest in a dream world, though Aries has what it takes to turn dreams into reality.

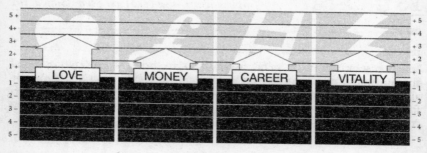

20 MONDAY
Moon Age Day 28   Moon Sign Aquarius

am...

pm...

The Sun is in your solar twelfth house at this time, encouraging a quieter interlude, and the real drive of this part of the year starts in a few weeks. This doesn't mean that you can't make any headway. Your best approach is to be fairly circumspect and to use mental ingenuity rather than brute force. At a creative level you are second to none.

21 TUESDAY
Moon Age Day 29   Moon Sign Aquarius

am...

pm...

New beginnings are on the cards, and as Venus acts as a herald to the Sun and Mercury in your solar first house, it is with relationships and especially with romance that the fun begins. By analysing the needs of loved ones you can also do yourself some good, and you tend to be right on the ball when it comes to your mental processes.

22 WEDNESDAY
Moon Age Day 0   Moon Sign Pisces

am...

pm...

In between bouts of activity you work at your best around now when you can retreat slightly into a different sort of reality. This is not really like Aries, and some people might wonder if there is something wrong with you. Be prepared to let them know that everything is fine, but that you are not really in the market for pushing yourself too hard.

23 THURSDAY
Moon Age Day 1   Moon Sign Pisces

am...

pm...

You can afford to push certain responsibilities into the background until the Sun moves on into your solar twelfth house. If you aren't firing on all cylinders in quite the way you normally would, this can lead to minor frustrations of one sort or another. Below the surface you should be as confident as ever and keeping things simmering.

24 FRIDAY

Moon Age Day 2   Moon Sign Pisces

am ....

pm ....

With the Moon in your solar twelfth house, you have scope to make this one of the quietest times of the month – at least for the first part of the day. Slowly but surely you should be ready to make the push that comes when the Moon moves into your own sign of Aries. By this evening the spotlight is on your vitality and your need to move.

25 SATURDAY

Moon Age Day 3   Moon Sign Aries

am ....

pm ....

Now you should be in a position to get things moving in the way you want. After all, you have been careful and patient for a few weeks. It could be that you will notice nature waking for the first time this year, but the real incentive right now is the lunar high, which positively insists you have a progressive and eventful weekend.

26 SUNDAY

Moon Age Day 4   Moon Sign Aries

am ....

pm ....

Your intuition has a great part to play in the way you view Sunday and in the way you act as a result. You have more scope to drive forward than has been the case for a while, but you may well need to apply the brakes once the new working week gets going. Today can be a practice for the more progressive phase that will be on offer quite soon.

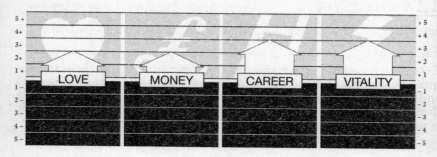

27 MONDAY
Moon Age Day 5   Moon Sign Taurus

m..

m..

Now your sensitivity is to the fore again and you can show just how caring and compassionate you are capable of being. The attention you have been giving to family and friends is certainly not wasted, and it helps you to prove to those around you that there is far more to Aries than the progressive, go-getting individual you sometimes are.

28 TUESDAY
Moon Age Day 6   Moon Sign Taurus

m..

m..

Trends indicate a possibility of some tricky finances to deal with, especially regarding business, or perhaps a family inheritance or other domestic issue. A day to be patient with anyone who doesn't fully understand the way things work, and to stay away from arguments that are not necessary and which won't solve anything at all.

29 WEDNESDAY
Moon Age Day 7   Moon Sign Taurus

m..

m..

It's leap year day, and with positive influences present in a romantic sense, if you want to pop the question, this would certainly be an ideal time to do so. On the other hand, you need to think carefully before you give too much away, because there is a slightly secretive side to your emotional nature and it is very much emphasised at present.

1 THURSDAY
Moon Age Day 8   Moon Sign Gemini

m..

m..

Certain events could now lead to feelings of escapism, which is actually quite unusual for Aries. Do you could feel slightly ill at ease with yourself and nowhere near as confidence as would normally be the case? If you don't know how to do something, remember that the best way forward is to ask someone who definitely does.

2 FRIDAY
Moon Age Day 9   Moon Sign Gemini

am...

pm...

It pays to sort out matters in personal relationships as soon as you can and you probably shouldn't allow issues to fester, simply because you don't want to address them. When things are out in the open they can be dealt with easily, but when they are under wraps nobody knows what is going on. In all work situations honesty is the best policy today.

3 SATURDAY
Moon Age Day 10   Moon Sign Cancer

am...

pm...

Your compassion and sympathy for others are now more highlighted than has been the case even during this quite sensitive period. Working on behalf of those who don't have either your confidence or your natural ability can really make the difference, and you can get a great deal out of providing a platform for those who are less capable to work from.

4 SUNDAY
Moon Age Day 11   Moon Sign Cancer

am...

pm...

Don't be surprised if you are constantly being influenced by others whilst the Sun occupies its present position. Of course this is true for all of us, but it might be something you are not used to. If you start doubting your own motivations or wondering what is going on inside you, just stand back and accept that you are deeper than you realised.

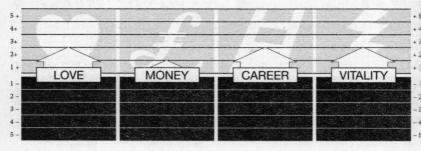

March

2012

YOUR MONTH AT A GLANCE

⊕ = Opportunities are around   ⊖ = Be on the defensive   ⬤ = Life is pretty ordinary

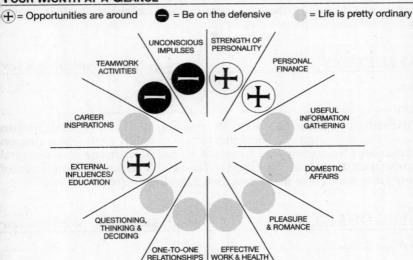

MARCH HIGHS AND LOWS

Here I show you how the rhythms of the Moon will affect you this month. Like the tide, your energies and abilities will rise and fall with its pattern. When it is above the centre line, go for it, when it is below, you should be resting.

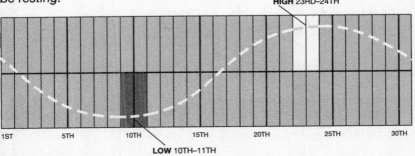

HIGH 23RD–24TH

LOW 10TH–11TH

63

5 MONDAY
Moon Age Day 12   Moon Sign Leo

am ....

pm ....

Are you feeling rather bored with your daily routines? If so, this would be a favourable time to make some subtle changes. Things are not quite right yet for the major alterations that are possible later in the month, but you can at least do some tinkering with your life. Confidence grows stronger, and others should prove helpful today.

6 TUESDAY
Moon Age Day 13   Moon Sign Leo

am ....

pm ....

Attracting new faces into your life could hardly be easier. You simply have to look around and there they are. Your ability to deal with money also counts for a great deal around now, and you can use it to improve your financial position. You might even be able to get certain people to recognise your worth more than they have done before.

7 WEDNESDAY
Moon Age Day 14   Moon Sign Leo

am ....

pm ....

A slightly introverted day is indicated, particularly if you are not quite as sure of yourself as would usually be the case. There is a low level of insecurity at work, influenced by those twelfth-house planets, and this is quite unusual for Aries. Keep pushing forward gently and trust in the fact that you are very capable.

8 THURSDAY
Moon Age Day 15   Moon Sign Virgo

am ....

pm ....

The Moon in your sixth house today is good for rational, sensible thought, but you still won't necessarily be putting yourself forward as much as is often the case. Why not get on top of any jobs that have been waiting for a while, and work away steadily towards your ultimate objectives? You might decide to pep up your social life in the evening.

9 FRIDAY
Moon Age Day 16   Moon Sign Virgo

am ....

pm...

There is likely to be a short interlude today during which you can once again display the more brash and go-getting side of Aries. Make the most of this, because with the lunar low coming along it pays to slow things down again tomorrow. If there is something you really want from life, today is a great time to ask for it.

10 SATURDAY
Moon Age Day 17   Moon Sign Libra

am ....

pm...

With the arrival of the lunar low, feelings of inadequacy and a little self-doubt are not out of the question, but you are so resilient by nature that you needn't allow these niggles to slow you down too much. With a great sense of your own worth starting to build, there is something of a battle going on inside you, and it's one you are certain to win.

11 SUNDAY
Moon Age Day 18   Moon Sign Libra

am ....

pm...

You shouldn't expect to move any mountains today, or even the odd small hill, come to that. Better by far for now to watch and wait. The lunar low marks the time each month when you can regenerate and bide your time. In a few days much of what is happening in your life should start to look more positive and quite different.

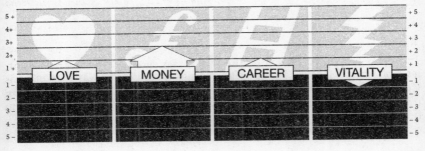

12 MONDAY ☿ *Moon Age Day 19   Moon Sign Scorpio*

am ....

pm ....

You are in a position to make important changes to yourself and your life today as the Moon moves on from its position in Libra. You stand at the edge of a significant crossroads, and it's worth seeking advice and support from others in order to make up your mind about the directions you are going to take in the longer term.

13 TUESDAY ☿ *Moon Age Day 20   Moon Sign Scorpio*

am ....

pm ....

Even if your influence over everyday life seems quite limited, take heart, because you are probably making much more progress than you realise. There are small gains to be made as far as your finances are concerned, and you can be quite charming when in social situations. Get out into the fresh air today, even if the weather is not good.

14 WEDNESDAY ☿ *Moon Age Day 21   Moon Sign Sagittarius*

am ....

pm ....

By taking a divergence from the usual well-trodden path of life you can open up new opportunities for personal and spiritual growth. It is important today not to always do the expected thing and to be willing to take the odd chance. In relationships you need to think about how you appear when seen through the eyes of others.

15 THURSDAY ☿ *Moon Age Day 22   Moon Sign Sagittarius*

am ....

pm ....

Trends assist you to be sharp and alert today, since this is the start of a new phase as Mercury starts to gee things up in your solar first house. Communication skills are well accented, and you may feel like a chrysalis turning into a butterfly. Capitalise on the fact that people are taking notice of you and that you can influence the world at large.

16 FRIDAY
☿ *Moon Age Day 23   Moon Sign Capricorn*

am ....

pm...

At work you have what it takes to be very enterprising, and it shouldn't take you long to make the sort of impression you would wish. Bear in mind that some of the plans you want to put into operation might unsettle those around you, and it is vital today that you explain yourself fully and that everyone understands your true motivations.

17 SATURDAY
☿ *Moon Age Day 24   Moon Sign Capricorn*

am ....

pm...

Misunderstandings will still be a distinct possibility for a day or so, and it would be particularly sensible at this time to make sure that loved ones know what you want – and why. Aries isn't always the best zodiac sign when it comes to keeping others informed, but if you are going to keep everyone happy you should at least try today.

18 SUNDAY
☿ *Moon Age Day 25   Moon Sign Capricorn*

am ....

pm...

Your personal magnetism is enhanced as the Moon moves into your solar eleventh house. Even if life isn't exactly electric, there is a strong hint that you can start to change things. Routines should seem less of a chore, and this is a Sunday during which you can find ways to have some fun and to entertain others on the way.

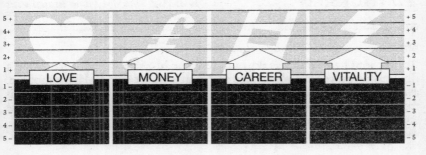

19 MONDAY ☿ *Moon Age Day 26   Moon Sign Aquarius*

am ....

pm ....

Communications are favoured, and you can get your message across in the way Aries does when at its best. Be prepared to rise to the challenge of additional responsibilities at work. If you are involved in higher education, breaking through barriers and making better progress is now the name of the game.

20 TUESDAY ☿ *Moon Age Day 27   Moon Sign Aquarius*

am ....

pm ....

Put ambitions aside for today and deal with the minutiae of life. If you get every little detail sorted out you should be ready for the big push that is coming. The current interlude calls for a good deal of self-examination, and you need to make certain that your motivations are sound and that you have your plans well laid.

21 WEDNESDAY ☿ *Moon Age Day 28   Moon Sign Pisces*

am ....

pm ....

Although there may be some fairly demanding duties to be dealt with today, it's a question of managing these with a smile and probably while whistling a little tune to yourself! Maybe you are noticing the arrival of the spring, or it could just be that a number of planetary influences are beginning to change, offering all sorts of new incentives.

22 THURSDAY ☿ *Moon Age Day 0   Moon Sign Pisces*

am ....

pm ....

Be prepared to slow things down today. The Moon is in your solar twelfth house and you can afford to tread water, at least for one day. By tomorrow everything is likely to seem different, and you need to be on top form to make the most of what the lunar high has in store for you. Why not spend some time with your lover today?

23 FRIDAY ☿ *Moon Age Day 1 Moon Sign Aries*

am ....

pm ....

Today your powers of persuasion are strong, and you shouldn't have any difficulty letting everyone know the way you feel about things. Financial luck is improved, and you may decide that this is the perfect period for taking a calculated risk of some sort. Just be careful you don't extend yourself too much in a social or romantic sense.

24 SATURDAY ☿ *Moon Age Day 2 Moon Sign Aries*

am ....

pm ....

Not only do you have the lunar high on your side today but at last the Sun has moved into your solar first house. Now the year should really begin to open up for you. With a host of new opportunities showing themselves in full colour, you can hardly avoid making this a special sort of day. This could be a weekend to remember.

25 SUNDAY ☿ *Moon Age Day 3 Moon Sign Taurus*

am ....

pm ....

Even if you are feeling extravagant, you don't have to spend a great deal of money in order to have fun. It is the free things in life that offer you the greatest opportunities right now, especially when you are in the company of people you really love. Speaking the right words romantically ought to be a piece of cake today.

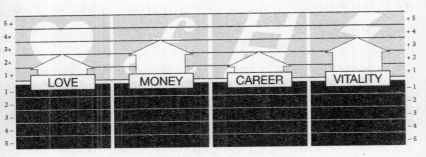

26 MONDAY ☿ *Moon Age Day 4   Moon Sign Tauru*

am ....

pm ....

There are signs that problems could arise at work if you are too impulsive
OK, so the planets are looking good for you, but that is no reason to go
off at a tangent or to try and do everything at once. It's worth slightly
repressing any feelings of excitement that are starting to grow inside you
at least for a few days. You can achieve everything eventually.

27 TUESDAY ☿ *Moon Age Day 5   Moon Sign Taurus*

am ....

pm ....

This would be a particularly favourable day for using your creativity to the
full. Self-expression is to the fore, and you should know instinctively how
to influence people in a really positive way. Most of what you gain today
comes from the direction of others, and the kinder and more appreciative
you are, the better things tend to get.

28 WEDNESDAY ☿ *Moon Age Day 6   Moon Sign Gemini*

am ....

pm ....

Confusion is a possibility for a few hours early today, particularly if there
are some details you have not checked, or changes to your routines that
you didn't expect. Fortunately, you are one of the best signs of the zodiac
when it comes to thinking on your feet, and you can make the best of
changing fortunes if you concentrate.

29 THURSDAY ☿ *Moon Age Day 7   Moon Sign Gemini*

am ....

pm ....

There could well be a little anger about today, especially when you are
dealing with people who frustrate you. Aries is not one to take prisoners
when it comes to getting what you want, and you don't like any sort of
interference. Unfortunately other people might also think they know the
best way forward, so compromise is the order of the day.

30 FRIDAY ☿ *Moon Age Day 8   Moon Sign Cancer*

am..

pm..

Today would be an ideal time to think about decorating or making other changes to your home surroundings that will make you feel more comfortable. Co-operation can work wonders in family matters, and the more everyone pulls together, the easier and more rewarding simple jobs are going to be. Be prepared for slight restrictions at work.

31 SATURDAY ☿ *Moon Age Day 9   Moon Sign Cancer*

am..

pm..

A day to balance your present emotions with your individuality. Sometimes you are inclined to forget that you can't always get just what you want at exactly the moment you desire it. A little patience would go a long way today, and you can be at your best when you sit and watch the river of life flow by for a few hours.

1 SUNDAY ☿ *Moon Age Day 10   Moon Sign Cancer*

am..

pm..

It's worth spending some time today doing things you know to be constructive. Exercise should also be a natural part of life now, perhaps in the company of your lover or a few good friends. You have what it takes to turn even chores into fun, and to find newer and better ways to convince everyone that your way forward is the best choice.

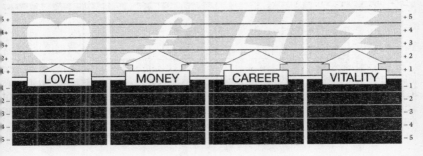

April

2012

YOUR MONTH AT A GLANCE

⊕ = Opportunities are around   ⊖ = Be on the defensive   ⬤ = Life is pretty ordinary

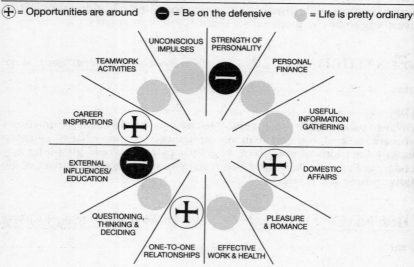

UNCONSCIOUS IMPULSES

STRENGTH OF PERSONALITY

TEAMWORK ACTIVITIES

PERSONAL FINANCE

CAREER INSPIRATIONS

USEFUL INFORMATION GATHERING

EXTERNAL INFLUENCES/ EDUCATION

DOMESTIC AFFAIRS

QUESTIONING, THINKING & DECIDING

PLEASURE & ROMANCE

ONE-TO-ONE RELATIONSHIPS

EFFECTIVE WORK & HEALTH

APRIL HIGHS AND LOWS

Here I show you how the rhythms of the Moon will affect you this month. Like the tide, your energies and abilities will rise and fall with its pattern. When it is above the centre line, go for it, when it is below, you should be resting.

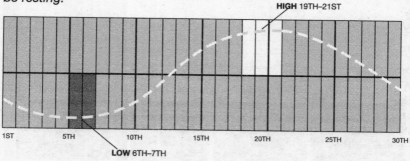

HIGH 19TH–21ST

LOW 6TH–7TH

1ST   5TH   10TH   15TH   20TH   25TH   30TH

2 MONDAY ☿ *Moon Age Day 11 Moon Sign Leo*

am ....

pm ....

This is a very favourable time to unearth new information and to get what you want from a whole host of situations. There is little to stand in your way now that the Sun is in your solar first house, and your energy and enthusiasm should certainly be evident. You have scope to make this a very good week indeed!

3 TUESDAY ☿ *Moon Age Day 12 Moon Sign Leo*

am ....

pm ....

Today is about identifying with others and getting onside with people you haven't been able to deal with easily in the past. There might be moments when you feel you have to stand up for yourself, but you needn't let these be a problem. You can afford to ooze confidence now, and it is unlikely that others would stand in your way.

4 WEDNESDAY ☿ *Moon Age Day 13 Moon Sign Virgo*

am ....

pm ....

The spotlight is on your efficiency at work and your ability to get things done in a fraction of the time colleagues can. This might get you noticed, usually for the right reasons, but occasionally for the wrong ones. Rubbing people up the wrong way is not helpful, so when you have done what you need to do, find ways to support others.

5 THURSDAY *Moon Age Day 14 Moon Sign Virgo*

am ....

pm ....

A positive frame of mind is encouraged as Venus races on into your solar third house. Communicating your feelings ought to be easy, especially at a romantic level, and the emphasis is on how attractive you can be to others. You set your own personal standards very high, so you shouldn't be surprised if others can't keep up.

6 FRIDAY

Moon Age Day 15   Moon Sign Libra

am ....

pm...

The lunar low is a time during which you might be tempted to over-extend yourself. This is not at all unusual for Aries when things are going well, and it's worth slowing life down a little, so that you can catch up with yourself. The weekend lies ahead and you should be planning something that is both exciting and ultimately profitable.

7 SATURDAY

Moon Age Day 16   Moon Sign Libra

am ....

pm...

Avoid getting yourself involved in anything risky while the lunar low is around. If you are scrupulous in your dealings with the world at large you should be able to avert problems, and in a general sense the pace of your life is such that you can coast through the lunar low without really noticing its presence too much.

8 SUNDAY

Moon Age Day 17   Moon Sign Scorpio

am ....

pm...

This would be a great time to find uses for old or ignored articles you thought you might never need again. The same is true for any ideas that you have previously put on hold, because they may now be relevant again. There is room for many people in your life at present, and your concern for both family members and friends is noteworthy.

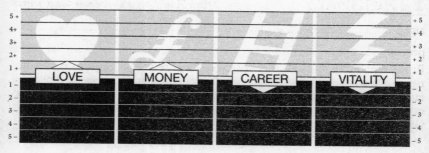

9 MONDAY
Moon Age Day 18   Moon Sign Scorpio

am ....

pm...

Opportunities for greater success may now lie in your professional life. This is a pivotal period of the year during which you can get most of what you want simply by being in the right place at the best time. If you can get people to listen to what you have to say and persuade them to take your ideas on board, that's half the battle.

10 TUESDAY
Moon Age Day 19   Moon Sign Sagittarius

am ....

pm...

Getting along with friends should be easy today, and Venus in its present position assists you to be sweetness and light to just about everyone. You can afford to look ahead a great deal just now, but there might also be a tendency for you to look back. There are lessons to be learned from the past, but they shouldn't prevent forward thinking.

11 WEDNESDAY
Moon Age Day 20   Moon Sign Sagittarius

am ....

pm...

A change to a current plan might turn out to be a good thing, and since you are the master of thinking on your feet you should be in an ideal position to pick up on unexpected opportunities. If you get onside with people you know are going to be successful, they are more likely to give you a tow towards your own objectives.

12 THURSDAY
Moon Age Day 21   Moon Sign Capricorn

am ....

pm...

Professional conflicts are possible today, thought they aren't really necessary and probably won't assist you in any way. It would be better by far right now to swallow your own pride and to get along with people, even though you can still be reasonably competitive. You need to ask yourself whether winning at all costs is likely to be the best policy.

13 FRIDAY

Moon Age Day 22   Moon Sign Capricorn

am ....

pm ....

A more optimistic time is available, and you have certainly come a long way since the beginning of this year. Don't bother yourself with pointless routines, and be willing to dump certain things that are no longer of any use to you. When it comes to romance you are presently in a good position to make the best possible impression.

14 SATURDAY

Moon Age Day 23   Moon Sign Aquarius

am ....

pm ....

You have everything you need to create a busy social life this weekend, even if there are also practical things you would wish to get done. Your sense of personal freedom is to the fore, and there are indications that you would fight hard to achieve your own objectives and to stay clear of anyone who wants to imprison you in some way.

15 SUNDAY

Moon Age Day 24   Moon Sign Aquarius

am ....

pm ....

It's time to tap into all the physical energy you possess and to use it in all sorts of different ways. Confidence to do the right thing remains very strong, and you may also be able to take the lead with a new idea that will fund your efforts for some weeks or months to come. Plan now for travel you are going to undertake later in the year.

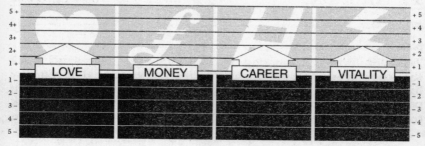

16 MONDAY
Moon Age Day 25   Moon Sign Aquarius

am ....

pm ....

Take care that overwork does not lead to mental exhaustion early this week. It's natural to want to keep moving forward, but you do tend to expect rather a lot of yourself. The response you can attract from those around you should be very positive, and you shouldn't have any trouble persuading other people to do some of the work for you.

17 TUESDAY
Moon Age Day 26   Moon Sign Pisces

am ....

pm ....

Once again your ability to convince those around you to listen to your views is emphasised, so it is therefore worth taking time out to explain yourself fully. You can even get people who have not been especially helpful in the past to rally round to offer assistance now, and you have a great capacity for keeping everyone working together.

18 WEDNESDAY
Moon Age Day 27   Moon Sign Pisces

am ....

pm ....

This is still a brand new period during which you can make progress in many different ways. Nevertheless, it is still worth taking some time out to think things through and to decide on the best course of action in each case. If you don't do this you could discover that there is a great deal of replication of effort taking place.

19 THURSDAY
Moon Age Day 28   Moon Sign Aries

am ....

pm ....

The Moon is back in your sign, assisting you to get things working out the way you wish. This would be an ideal time to give your romantic life a boost, even if it has been going fairly well anyway. It is within your power to change the way others see you, and it's worth showing them the potential within you that they may not have noticed before.

20 FRIDAY

Moon Age Day 29   Moon Sign Aries

am ....

pm..

Your optimism and interest should be there for all to see. This has potential to be an extremely full day, and there are opportunities to follow a course of action that might have been blocked to you before. It would take someone extremely clever to pull the wool over your eyes right now, and you have a chance to prosper in most areas of life.

21 SATURDAY

Moon Age Day 0   Moon Sign Aries

am ....

pm..

For the third day running the Moon remains in your own zodiac sign of Aries, which extends the generally positive trends into the weekend. Try to do something different today, and if possible stay away from the sort of routines you have to follow on weekdays. In particular, there is an emphasis on having fun, perhaps alongside friends.

22 SUNDAY

Moon Age Day 1   Moon Sign Taurus

am ....

pm..

Getting your message across to others could prove to be extremely important at the moment, so it's vital you make sure they are at least listening to what you have to say. Finding an attentive audience is certainly not difficult when you are so charismatic and good to know. You would be wise to avoid arguments at all costs right now.

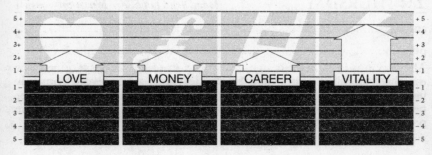

23 MONDAY   *Moon Age Day 2   Moon Sign Taurus*

am ....

pm ....

Mercury in its present position gives you everything you need to thrive in social situations and you can turn your ready wit to good ends, especially at work. Once again it's about getting people to listen to what you are saying and letting the light of your personality shine out. Beware of appearing to be too pushy today.

24 TUESDAY   *Moon Age Day 3   Moon Sign Gemini*

am ....

pm ....

Social affairs and positive encounters with others continue to be of supreme importance to you at this time. The way you come across to the world at large is very important because it sets the seal on how much help and support you can gain from those around you in the weeks ahead. Show the really charming side of your nature.

25 WEDNESDAY   *Moon Age Day 4   Moon Sign Gemini*

am ....

pm ....

Mars is now in your solar sixth house and so acting rashly could turn out to be disadvantageous to you. It would be far better right now to think things through before you take any particular sort of action. You need to be ruled by your head and not your heart and to show all the common sense you are capable of mustering.

26 THURSDAY   *Moon Age Day 5   Moon Sign Gemini*

am ....

pm ....

All mental pursuits are favoured today and you have the chance to show everyone around you just how ingenious you are capable of being. By using a logical approach you might be able to dream up a newer and better way of doing something that hasn't changed for years. You have scope to make this the start of a fairly profitable period.

27 FRIDAY
Moon Age Day 6   Moon Sign Cancer

am ....

pm ....

Commercial issues are well accented today and you should be right on the ball when it comes to any sort of business deal. While others stand around and think, you need to be pitching in and making things happen. This is also an ideal day for any form of travel and for making gains as a result of meeting strangers – especially those from far away.

28 SATURDAY
Moon Age Day 7   Moon Sign Cancer

am ....

pm ....

There could well be great changes coming along for you in a personal sense, though you needn't allow these to work against your best interests. On the contrary, romantic attachments can be strengthened, and it's worth making the most of the chance to start a new relationship at any time now – that is, if you have been looking for one!

29 SUNDAY
Moon Age Day 8   Moon Sign Leo

am ....

pm ....

It's natural to want to be admired and appreciated by everyone, and you have the chance to really shine on this particular Sunday. It is very important to Aries to know that you are at the centre of people's thoughts, but there shouldn't be much doubt about that at the moment. If routines don't seem inviting, why not leave them alone?

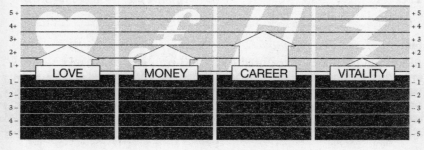

30 MONDAY

Moon Age Day 9   Moon Sign Leo

am ....

pm...

All monetary matters and investments are highlighted at the moment, and you have scope to discover new ways to make money that you didn't really think about before. There is much to be said for devoting time to planning your financial strategy, and also for associating with people who think very much the way you do.

1 TUESDAY

Moon Age Day 10 · Moon Sign Virgo

am ....

pm...

Practical duties could prove to be something of a bind at the beginning of May. That's a shame, because in other respects you can make the world your oyster. Perhaps you can convince other people to do some of the routine jobs, while you look forward and make longer-term plans. In social settings you have a chance to shine like a star today.

2 WEDNESDAY

Moon Age Day 11 · Moon Sign Virgo

am ....

pm...

Travel, communication and other mental as well as social connections with people are emphasised for you right now. Gathering new information and getting the benefit of sound advice is also to be recommended. Even if not all the advice you do receive seems sensible at first, you need to think about it for a while before deciding.

3 THURSDAY

Moon Age Day 12   Moon Sign Virgo

am ....

pm...

Slowing things down a little would be no bad thing today. The spotlight is on family concerns and on your desires to get others, especially young people, to do what you think they should. You need to be ready to deal with any obstacles you encounter, and to bear in mind that you won't necessarily make the progress that has been possible recently.

4 FRIDAY
Moon Age Day 13   Moon Sign Libra

am...

pm...

The reason for the slight setbacks and delays now becomes obvious. The lunar low could make certain aspects of life seem like swimming through treacle. One option is for you to leave issues alone that can't be resolved quickly, and you should probably avoid getting involved in pointless arguments about matters that are not at all important.

5 SATURDAY
Moon Age Day 14   Moon Sign Libra

am...

pm...

The start of the weekend might not seem all that wonderful, particularly if you are hedged in by family duties or by jobs you have been putting off because you have been so busy recently. Find some way to reward yourself for all your recent efforts and instead of trying to move forward, be content to stay where you are for today.

6 SUNDAY
Moon Age Day 15   Moon Sign Scorpio

am...

pm...

A day to avoid family discussions that you know are going to turn into arguments, and instead of staying at home, to try to get out and about, perhaps in the company of your lover or friends. Aries now has scope to capitalise on a new romantic interlude, and this is also an excellent time to appreciate the achievements of others.

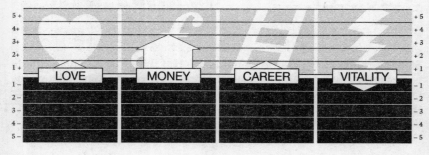

May

2012

YOUR MONTH AT A GLANCE

⊕ = Opportunities are around   ⊖ = Be on the defensive   ⚪ = Life is pretty ordinary

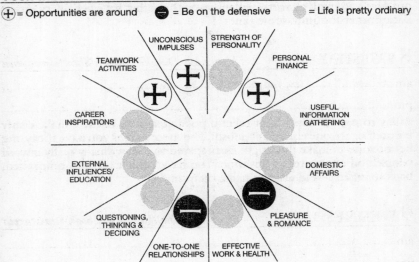

UNCONSCIOUS IMPULSES

STRENGTH OF PERSONALITY

TEAMWORK ACTIVITIES

PERSONAL FINANCE

CAREER INSPIRATIONS

USEFUL INFORMATION GATHERING

EXTERNAL INFLUENCES/ EDUCATION

DOMESTIC AFFAIRS

QUESTIONING, THINKING & DECIDING

PLEASURE & ROMANCE

ONE-TO-ONE RELATIONSHIPS

EFFECTIVE WORK & HEALTH

MAY HIGHS AND LOWS

Here I show you how the rhythms of the Moon will affect you this month. Like the tide, your energies and abilities will rise and fall with its pattern. When it is above the centre line, go for it, when it is below, you should be resting.

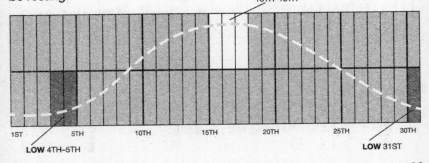

16TH–18TH

1ST   5TH   10TH   15TH   20TH   25TH   30TH

LOW 4TH–5TH

LOW 31ST

7 MONDAY
Moon Age Day 16   Moon Sign Scorpio

am...

pm...

A bright and breezy attitude to life suits today's influences, and such an approach will allow you to take most things in your stride. This ought to be the start of a fairly positive week for Aries, and you should be able to push forward with all sorts of plans, even those that have been kept on the back burner for quite some time.

8 TUESDAY
Moon Age Day 17   Moon Sign Sagittarius

am...

pm...

A day to opt for some light relief if possible and to refuse to take either yourself or anyone else too seriously. The more laughs you have today, the better you can make things go. Be prepared to deal with any really intense people you encounter at this time. You have what it takes to bring them back to reality – and even to make them smile!

9 WEDNESDAY
Moon Age Day 18   Moon Sign Sagittarius

am...

pm...

The spotlight is now on the influence you have on your employer and on work in general, and you should bear this in mind if you have been looking for a pay rise or any sort of advancement. There is much to be said for welcoming people you haven't seen for ages back into your life, and for making the most of any new incentives they bring.

10 THURSDAY
Moon Age Day 19   Moon Sign Capricorn

am...

pm...

It's time to capitalise on positive trends regarding investments, or possible associated with a plan you have been mulling over. Whatever you are doing today, make sure you bring a fresh and happy attitude to life, which could well be noticed by those around you. It's also important to make sure you are looking after yourself physically.

11 FRIDAY

Moon Age Day 20   Moon Sign Capricorn

am...

pm...

All travel and communication is positively highlighted. Venus remains in your solar third house, assisting you to keep relationships working well and to make a very positive impression on others. Rather than staying in the same place all day, your interests are best served by moving around.

12 SATURDAY

Moon Age Day 21   Moon Sign Aquarius

am...

pm...

Improved communications mean that you should have no trouble letting others know exactly how you feel about any kind of situation. This doesn't indicate that you have to be in any way critical or grumpy in your approach. On the contrary, you seem to have what it takes to be charming to everyone, and this will have a bearing on the reactions you get.

13 SUNDAY

Moon Age Day 22   Moon Sign Aquarius

am...

pm...

Your imagination and sensitivity are stimulated by the present position of the Moon in your solar chart. There is just a slight chance that you may decide it's necessary to withdraw from specific situations, especially if you feel as though too much is being expected of you. Stand by for a quieter couple of days, though this needn't be a dull time.

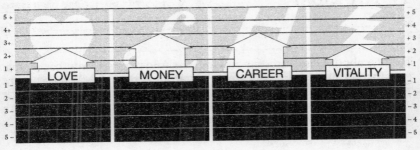

14 MONDAY

Moon Age Day 23   Moon Sign Pisces

am..

pm..

Ahead of the lunar high it sometimes happens that people feel as though the brakes of life are being slightly applied. This could easily be the case for you at this time, but if you look at life you will see that the one who is in control of slowing things down is you. It is impossible to live at full speed all the time, and you need moments to reflect.

15 TUESDAY

Moon Age Day 24   Moon Sign Pisces

am..

pm..

You always have very high goals, so much so that you expect a great deal of yourself. That's fine, just as long as you realise that you are human and that not everything will always work out exactly as you would wish. Don't be afraid of eating eat a slice of humble pie if required today, and even if you don't like the taste, it won't do you any harm.

16 WEDNESDAY

Moon Age Day 25   Moon Sign Aries

am..

pm..

Positive trends are definitely around you now. The Moon is back in your zodiac sign, and it's all hands to action stations! This has potential to be the busiest part of this week, particularly if you are willing to make yourself the centre of attention. You have scope to be number one in social settings, and can use this to your definite advantage.

17 THURSDAY

Moon Age Day 26   Moon Sign Aries

am..

pm..

Today is about being assertive and letting those closest to you know what you intend to do, and how soon you want to get started. You should be able to persuade people to follow your lead when you are in this frame of mind, and you can also be charming, which definitely helps. Trends indicate a slight restlessness at home.

18 FRIDAY

Moon Age Day 27   Moon Sign Aries

am ....

pm ....

The lunar high is still around as today gets going, but as the hours wear on the emphasis moves to your desire for some sort of comfort. Whether this means you will be buying bars of chocolate or a new mattress remains to be seen, but by the evening you may revel in the chance to just put your feet up.

19 SATURDAY

Moon Age Day 28   Moon Sign Taurus

am ....

pm ....

Trends suggest you may now no longer be willing to accept the status quo, because the level of your ambition is going off the scale. Making changes is the order of the day, whether others like it or not. If standard responses in conversations with others don't seem to work today, you could discover that you need to be slightly ingenious.

20 SUNDAY

Moon Age Day 0   Moon Sign Taurus

am ....

pm ....

Today sees a strong focus on building up your personal resources. There are good reasons to take an hour or two to think about things and to make very definite plans about the way you are going to approach finances in the weeks ahead. In some respects you can turn this into a pivotal and very important period.

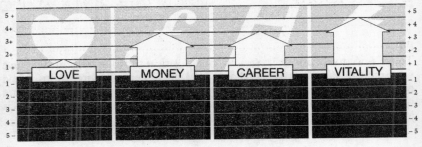

21 MONDAY
Moon Age Day 1   Moon Sign Gemini

am ....

pm...

You can afford to express more intellectual confidence this week and to show that in most situations you know what you are talking about and can speak confidently on your own behalf. You should also be prepared to stick up for anyone you think may be getting a raw deal in some way. Why not get out and about when you are not too busy?

22 TUESDAY
Moon Age Day 2   Moon Sign Gemini

am ....

pm...

It could well seem as though there is so much happening around you that is interesting, that it's difficult to know exactly what to get on with first. A plan of action may be necessary, but that shouldn't be difficult for you. This would also be a good time to turn your attention to any family matters that you haven't considered seriously enough before.

23 WEDNESDAY
Moon Age Day 3   Moon Sign Gemini

am ....

pm...

Don't be afraid to seek support from family members and possibly from older people especially. Aries always wants to prove things for itself, but a degree of experience helps and you can sometimes avoid making a particular mistake by talking to someone who has been in a situation before. It pays to be careful what you eat at present.

24 THURSDAY
Moon Age Day 4   Moon Sign Cancer

am ....

pm...

There's no doubt about it, you are in a position to think on your feet and to make the sort of progress that would have seemed quite impossible a month or two ago. If it seems that there is still more you need to do, it's worth exercising a little patience and making certain that you approach jobs one at once, otherwise a muddle could ensue.

25 FRIDAY
Moon Age Day 5   Moon Sign Cancer

am ....

pm...

Travel is well highlighted in your solar chart, and there are incentives galore on offer. In reality you could be spoiled for choice, and if so there's nothing wrong with choosing those things that benefit others as much as they please you. Showing your partner how much you care about them can work wonders, even if you have a limited amount of time to do so.

26 SATURDAY
Moon Age Day 6   Moon Sign Leo

am ....

pm...

Trends encourage you to stay alongside friends this weekend and to drop some of the responsibility for a day or two. You work very hard and so you sometimes feel the need to play hard too. In quieter moments you can look inside and see the person living in there that doesn't always get out into the fresh air. Meditation is always necessary.

27 SUNDAY
Moon Age Day 7   Moon Sign Leo

am ....

pm...

All communication matters remain rewarding, the more so now that the Sun has entered your solar third house. This is a time during which you have a chance to tell others how you really feel, whilst at the same time being extremely entertaining and quite funny. Treat today as a holiday and make sure you don't work if you can avoid doing so.

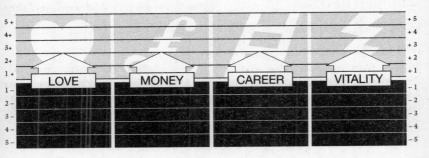

28 MONDAY
Moon Age Day 8   Moon Sign Leo

am ....

pm ....

A day to keep abreast of current news, in case something that is happening out there in the wider world has a strong bearing on your own life. This is a time to act with courage and confidence and to show others, especially your boss, that you are up for a challenge and quite willing to go that extra yard if necessary.

29 TUESDAY
Moon Age Day 9   Moon Sign Virgo

am ....

pm ....

During this period it's important to find plenty of energy to put into practical matters. When others drop by the side of the road with fatigue, you should still be pushing on at full speed. Any situation that sorts out the wheat from the chaff is good for you under present trends, though even you need to be slightly careful of fatigue.

30 WEDNESDAY
Moon Age Day 10   Moon Sign Virgo

am ....

pm ....

Once again it is important to mention that you need to make adequate time for rest and relaxation. By tomorrow the lunar low will have arrived, and carrying on at breakneck speed is not to be recommended. That's why it would be sensible today to look ahead at a two-day period during which you should be thinking and not acting.

31 THURSDAY
Moon Age Day 11   Moon Sign Libra

am ....

pm ....

Cool, calm and relaxed – that's what you need to be if you are going to enjoy, rather than endure, the lunar low this month. Pushing against situations is not your best option right now, and you may as well get used to the fact right from the start. Be willing to watch and wait, while offering more of the running to those around you.

1 FRIDAY
Moon Age Day 12   Moon Sign Libra

am ....

pm...

Learning how to delegate is part of the lesson that Aries has to learn in life. This is as good a time as any to let others have their head. You can be proud that you have taught people so well, not only in a work setting but probably with younger people at home. By the end of today you can start to speed things up again, which should please you.

2 SATURDAY
Moon Age Day 13   Moon Sign Scorpio

am ....

pm...

The negative side of having Mars in your solar sixth house can be an inflated ego. From your side of the fence it looks as though you know what you are doing and are willing to say so. Remember that when viewed from a different perspective it might appear that you are showing off, or maybe even belittling slightly less dynamic types.

3 SUNDAY
Moon Age Day 14   Moon Sign Scorpio

am ....

pm...

It ought to be easier now to express yourself in an emotional sense. Venus remains in your solar third house, from where it has offered you a positive influence for a month or more. In particular it encourages you to take a sympathetic approach, and to verbalise your sympathy. Sometimes Aries fails to make its true depth and sensitivity known.

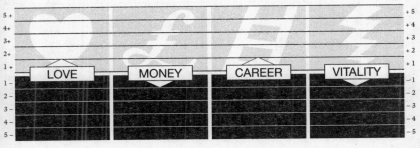

June

2012

YOUR MONTH AT A GLANCE

$\oplus$ = Opportunities are around $\ominus$ = Be on the defensive   ⬤ = Life is pretty ordinary

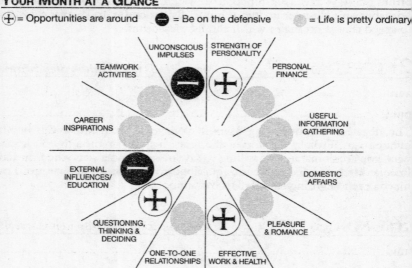

- UNCONSCIOUS IMPULSES
- STRENGTH OF PERSONALITY
- TEAMWORK ACTIVITIES
- PERSONAL FINANCE
- CAREER INSPIRATIONS
- USEFUL INFORMATION GATHERING
- EXTERNAL INFLUENCES/ EDUCATION
- DOMESTIC AFFAIRS
- QUESTIONING, THINKING & DECIDING
- PLEASURE & ROMANCE
- ONE-TO-ONE RELATIONSHIPS
- EFFECTIVE WORK & HEALTH

JUNE HIGHS AND LOWS

Here I show you how the rhythms of the Moon will affect you this month. Like the tide, your energies and abilities will rise and fall with its pattern. When it is above the centre line, go for it, when it is below, you should be resting.

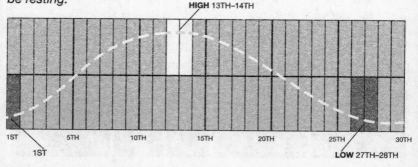

HIGH 13TH–14TH

LOW 27TH–28TH

1ST   5TH   10TH   15TH   20TH   25TH   30TH

1ST

4 MONDAY
Moon Age Day 15   Moon Sign Sagittarius

am ....

pm...

This is a period during which you can use things that are going on in the outside world to lift your spirits no end. There are gains to be made from being in the right place at the right time, and your enthusiasm to do something new is to the fore. You should also be ready to identify potentials you might have completely missed before.

5 TUESDAY
Moon Age Day 16   Moon Sign Sagittarius

am ....

pm...

By all means use your wit, planning and determination to push on with your special plans, but at the same time be prepared to listen to what colleagues are saying. They might have recognised something you have overlooked, which you can incorporate into your own way forward. Love looks especially favoured once work is out of the way.

6 WEDNESDAY
Moon Age Day 17   Moon Sign Capricorn

am ....

pm...

Professional developments remain generally positive and you have what it takes to be very convincing when you are dealing with those people around you that have influence. You are encouraged to be just slightly careful regarding your health at the moment, because you could be more prone to minor ailments than would normally be the case.

7 THURSDAY
Moon Age Day 18   Moon Sign Capricorn

am ....

pm...

When it comes to the task at hand, don't allow your ego to get in the way. It is more important to get things done than to worry whether or not you are receiving personal accolades. Aries can be quite selfless on occasions, but at the moment there are signs that you want everyone to notice you. A good effort now will pay off later.

8 FRIDAY

Moon Age Day 19   Moon Sign Aquarius

am ....

pm ....

Highly intellectual pursuits could be right up your street at the end of this working week. There is also an emphasis on stimulating entertainment, so this would be an ideal time to take yourself off to the theatre or to a concert. Persuading other people to help you out with a prospective weekend project might not be as easy as you thought.

9 SATURDAY

Moon Age Day 20   Moon Sign Aquarius

am ....

pm ....

This is a day for positivity and optimism, and this is a reflection of that third-house Venus that has been helping you along for a number of weeks now. What really counts is the way you talk to others and what they take from the conversation. Bear in mind that you could be doing yourself a great deal of good in the medium and long term.

10 SUNDAY

Moon Age Day 21   Moon Sign Pisces

am ....

pm ....

There are signs that your imagination could be working overtime on this particular Sunday, which can be both a blessing and a curse. New ideas come thick and fast, but you could also be faced with potential pitfalls that don't really exist at all. It is important to take a realistic view of life and to weight up pros and cons sensibly.

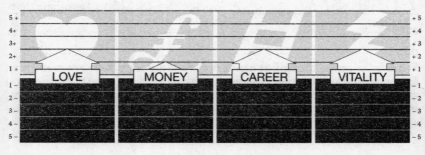

11 MONDAY
Moon Age Day 22   Moon Sign Pisces

am ....

pm ....

Family matters are positively highlighted, though today and tomorrow a quieter and less reactive approach works best in a general sense. This is because the Moon presently occupies your solar twelfth house, encouraging you to slow down and become more reflective. Beware of ruffling feathers unnecessarily today.

12 TUESDAY
Moon Age Day 23   Moon Sign Pisces

am ....

pm ....

You can afford to tread water in some situations, and it might be sensible not to take any really important decisions until tomorrow if you can avoid doing so. Things could come to light that will change your mind at the eleventh hour, and in any case your practical common sense is inclined to guide you towards the lunar high.

13 WEDNESDAY
Moon Age Day 24   Moon Sign Aries

am ....

pm ....

If you have been dependent on other people for your support, this would be an excellent time to strike out on your own. Physical energy counts for a great deal while the lunar high is around, and Aries is now just about as potent as any zodiac sign could be. Pushing through previously insurmountable obstacles is what today is all about.

14 THURSDAY
Moon Age Day 25   Moon Sign Aries

am ....

pm ....

Stand by to make this a high point in terms of maintaining your progress in life generally. Your energy levels remain emphasised, assisting you to be active and enterprising throughout the whole of today. Even when you are not working you have scope to make things happen, and to positively exhaust other people, just by being around!

15 FRIDAY   *Moon Age Day 26   Moon Sign Taurus*

am..

pm..

Conversations with others should go smoothly enough at the moment, and at least you are standing still long enough to hear what they have to say in reply. You can create a harmonious sort of give and take between yourself and family members, and this would be an ideal time to heal any breach that has existed for a while.

16 SATURDAY   *Moon Age Day 27   Moon Sign Taurus*

am..

pm..

Reasonable gains could be on offer as far as money is concerned. This might relate to actions you took in the past, but also to the sensible way you are able to view things at the moment. It is towards the medium term that you should be looking today, and there is less emphasis on what you can achieve right at this exact moment.

17 SUNDAY   *Moon Age Day 28   Moon Sign Taurus*

am..

pm..

There's nothing wrong with being willing to fight for what you want, and this is a reflection of the present position of Mars in your solar chart. But that doesn't mean this is the right thing to do on every occasion. There are times today when you will achieve a great deal more by using psychology rather than brute force. Think before you speak out.

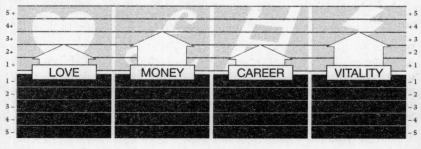

18 MONDAY

Moon Age Day 29   Moon Sign Gemini

am ....

pm ....

The focus is on your mercurial gift of the gab around this time and people should find you interesting to have around. Even strangers could be on the receiving end of your need for conversation, and you might be able to make some new friends as a result of different social activities. Don't rule things out today, but be open to suggestion.

19 TUESDAY

Moon Age Day 0   Moon Sign Gemini

am ....

pm ....

There are signs that the domestic scene could be getting far busier than it was even a few weeks ago. Maybe there is just a lot going on in the family, or it could be that you have decided to make significant changes within your home. Whatever the reason, your own four walls and the people within them are now under the spotlight.

20 WEDNESDAY

Moon Age Day 1   Moon Sign Cancer

am ....

pm ....

Once again, all things domestic have potential to be both important and fulfilling. This doesn't mean you have to ignore the more practical, work-based area of life, though there's nothing wrong with 'coasting' for a few days in a career sense. Showing others you are proud of them should be a natural aspect of life now.

21 THURSDAY

Moon Age Day 2   Moon Sign Cancer

am ....

pm ....

At this time it can be said that home is where the heart is. There are a number of fourth-house planetary associations that are becoming stronger in your chart, encouraging you to look at your domestic circumstances and to spend more time in the company of family members. Love should be especially warm and welcoming now.

22 FRIDAY
Moon Age Day 3   Moon Sign Cancer

am ....

pm ....

Extremely high energy levels could motivate you to turn back towards the outside world, and as a result there may well be a conflict developing within you. The way forward is to employ a sensible balance between the different things you have to do. In some ways you work best alone for the next couple of days, though you needn't be standoffish.

23 SATURDAY
Moon Age Day 4   Moon Sign Leo

am ....

pm ....

There is now a strong emphasis on your ego, which isn't too unusual for Aries. It is important to believe in yourself, but not to the extent that you alienate others. The more humble you appear, the greater is the chance that other people will like you more and want to be of assistance. You may decide to back an underdog today.

24 SUNDAY
Moon Age Day 5   Moon Sign Leo

am ....

pm ....

You are in a position to keep relationships smooth today, especially with people at home. At the same time romance is well accented, assisting you to make words of love trip from your tongue as if you were a poet. It's time to show your appreciation, and you can do so in a number of both practical and frivolous ways.

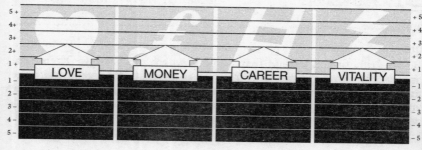

25 MONDAY
Moon Age Day 6   Moon Sign Virgo

am ....

pm ....

Mercury is now in your solar fourth house, reinforcing the emphasis on your home during this part of June. There are good reasons to keep your immediate environs uppermost in your mind, and you might even decide to do something fairly spectacular in your garden. Watch out for muscular strains and sprains!

26 TUESDAY
Moon Age Day 7   Moon Sign Virgo

am ....

pm ....

Armed with even more energy and enthusiasm, this is the part of the week when you should be making every move count and when you can get those around you on board and working alongside you. It's a question of knowing at every stage what you should be doing and what is likely to happen. Some might call you psychic.

27 WEDNESDAY
Moon Age Day 8   Moon Sign Libra

am ....

pm ....

Stand by to make the best of a quieter couple of days and accept the fact that when the lunar low is around you shouldn't be moving any mountains. In all probability you won't want to do so, and if you are willing to meditate for a while you can make this a warm and wonderful time. It isn't what happens that counts, but how you use the influences.

28 THURSDAY
Moon Age Day 9   Moon Sign Libra

am ....

pm ....

Be prepared to deal with setbacks and delays that you could encounter at any time today. Changes might have to be made with regard to planned journeys, and you may not be able to count on people to quite the extent you would wish. There is much to be said for going with the flow and accepting that everything is going to turn out fine in the end.

29 FRIDAY
Moon Age Day 10   Moon Sign Scorpio

am...

pm...

Be willing to readjust your plans today. Although the lunar low has passed you do have the Moon in your solar eighth house, which indicates that things could change at a moment's notice. The real difference now is that you can make any alterations that do take place work very much to your advantage. Energy still counts for a great deal.

30 SATURDAY
Moon Age Day 11   Moon Sign Scorpio

am...

pm...

Beware of going ahead with anything for which you have not laid definite foundations. Your ego reappears, and could get you into trouble unless you control it somewhat. There are good reasons to show everyone just how willing you are to compromise and to co-operate, and this will help you to avoid making enemies.

1 SUNDAY
Moon Age Day 12   Moon Sign Sagittarius

am...

pm...

The Moon has now moved on and from its present position it points towards travel. It's time to broaden your horizons, either for business or for pleasure, and in fact you might be able to find ways today to serve both. Getting on well with colleagues can help you to bring at least some of them to a more prominent position in your social life.

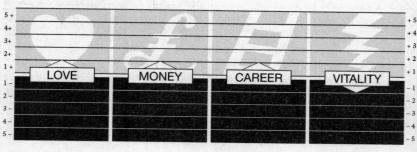

July

2012

YOUR MONTH AT A GLANCE

⊕ = Opportunities are around   ⊖ = Be on the defensive   ◯ = Life is pretty ordinary

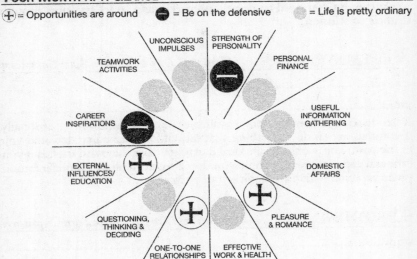

STRENGTH OF PERSONALITY

UNCONSCIOUS IMPULSES

PERSONAL FINANCE

TEAMWORK ACTIVITIES

USEFUL INFORMATION GATHERING

CAREER INSPIRATIONS

DOMESTIC AFFAIRS

EXTERNAL INFLUENCES/ EDUCATION

PLEASURE & ROMANCE

QUESTIONING, THINKING & DECIDING

EFFECTIVE WORK & HEALTH

ONE-TO-ONE RELATIONSHIPS

JULY HIGHS AND LOWS

Here I show you how the rhythms of the Moon will affect you this month. Like the tide, your energies and abilities will rise and fall with its pattern. When it is above the centre line, go for it, when it is below, you should be resting.

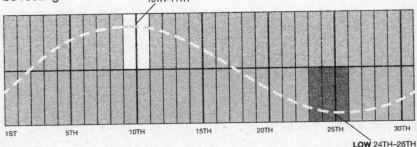

10TH–11TH

1ST   5TH   10TH   15TH   20TH   25TH   30TH

LOW 24TH–26TH

2 MONDAY
Moon Age Day 13   Moon Sign Sagittarius

am ....

pm...

Be careful today and be willing to slow things down a little. Mars is not presently in the best position for you, and it brings the possibility of a few mistakes. You should be able to find plenty of time to do everything this week, though you need to be well prepared, and to follow jobs through to their conclusion.

3 TUESDAY
Moon Age Day 14   Moon Sign Capricorn

am ....

pm...

A strong sense of achievement is available to you at the moment, especially if you manage to do something that has either puzzled or defeated you in the past. This would be an ideal day to get together with friends if you can, and especially with people you don't see very often. There are good times on offer, with pals or with your partner.

4 WEDNESDAY
Moon Age Day 15   Moon Sign Capricorn

am ....

pm...

If some communications seem a little strained, you will have to work so much harder today to get your message across. Does it appear that people around you are taking offence at the slightest thing? That might be so, though you also need to remember that you may not be at your most diplomatic under present planetary trends.

5 THURSDAY
Moon Age Day 16   Moon Sign Capricorn

am ....

pm...

This is most likely the best day of the week for dealing with all contingencies at home. Today is all about getting on well with those closest to you and persuading them to listen to what you have to say. Whether or not you can also convince them to follow your lead remains to be seen, so beware of expecting too much.

6 FRIDAY
Moon Age Day 17   Moon Sign Aquarius

am ....

pm ....

The Moon is now in your solar eleventh house and that allows you to put yourself in the social mainstream. Love is favoured, especially for Aries people who have recently embarked on a new relationship, and you seem to have what it takes to sweep someone off their feet. Stay away from gossip or rumours, which could turn out to be groundless.

7 SATURDAY
Moon Age Day 18   Moon Sign Aquarius

am ....

pm ....

You need to beware of shady types at this stage of the week, and especially anyone who seems to be offering something for nothing. In truth, nothing is what you will probably end up with, and so it pays to be scrupulous in any sort of financial dealings. Beware of parting with cash this weekend unless you are certain of what you'll get in return.

8 SUNDAY
Moon Age Day 19   Moon Sign Pisces

am ....

pm ....

This is a time for creating harmony and serenity in your relationships with the world at large. It's a question of staying well away from arguments, though you should be willing to step in and pour oil on troubled waters. It's time to show younger family members just how ageless you are.

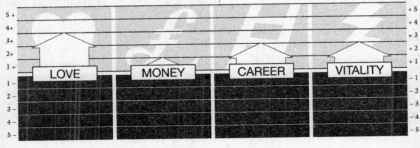

9 MONDAY
Moon Age Day 20   Moon Sign Pisces

am ....

pm ....

Compromise could be your weak point today. The fact is that if you know you are correct, you won't want to give any ground at all. Aries can be rather stubborn on occasions, and with the planets the way they are, that's a distinct possibility now. All the same, there are times when you need to share, and today is such a time.

10 TUESDAY
Moon Age Day 21   Moon Sign Aries

am ....

pm ....

You have great opportunities to put yourself forward while the lunar high is around, and you can ensure that this is a significant turning point in the month. If you have been seeking to advance your career, now is the time to get going. At the same time you can afford to be very sociable and ready to make the most of anything on offer.

11 WEDNESDAY
Moon Age Day 22   Moon Sign Aries

am ....

pm ....

Self-confidence is the order of the day, and you have what it takes to go through life with a definite smile at the moment. There's nothing wrong with taking a chance or two, especially when it comes to finances, and you might also be able to benefit as a result of efforts you put in earlier in the year. An ideal day for getting out and about.

12 THURSDAY
Moon Age Day 23   Moon Sign Taurus

am ....

pm ....

As long as Venus remains where it is in your solar chart this has potential to be a period of change. This is a favourable time to make new friends and acquaintances, and some Aries subjects might even decide on a change of career, or be dealing with upheavals in their present job. Don't simply take all this in your stride – enjoy it!

13 FRIDAY · · · · · · · · · · · · · *Moon Age Day 24 · · Moon Sign Taurus*

am..

pm...

Your domestic life should now offer rewards. Maybe this is because on Friday the 13th you think it's safer to stay at home. If there is any bad luck about, you needn't allow it to affect you too much. On the contrary, you have scope to make the most of some fairly profitable opportunities that are available around now.

14 SATURDAY · · · · · · · · *Moon Age Day 25 · · Moon Sign Taurus*

am..

pm...

Trends bring the possibility of a few power battles relating to who is actually in charge in a particular relationship. You don't always give ground very easily, but you can afford to be slightly more flexible this weekend than would usually be the case. This doesn't mean you are being weak, merely that you are better able to find compromises.

15 SUNDAY · · · · · · · ☿ · · *Moon Age Day 26 · · Moon Sign Gemini*

am..

pm...

Creativity is much enhanced by the changing position of Mercury in your solar chart. Now you can structure that powerful imagination and make the most of new happenings to show how easily you rise to a given situation. Romance is also moving to the fore, so it's time to make sure you have some attention coming your way.

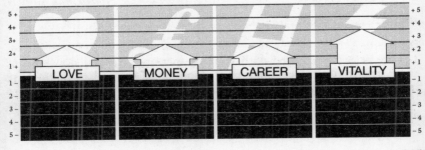

16 MONDAY ☿ *Moon Age Day 27   Moon Sign Gemini*

am ....

pm ....

Handling several different tasks at the same time shouldn't be difficult for Aries people today. The Moon is in a strong position for you, and you should also find it easier than normal to verbalise your emotions. Offering words of love can make all the difference, and can help you to make those around you feel very safe and secure.

17 TUESDAY ☿ *Moon Age Day 28   Moon Sign Gemini*

am ....

pm ....

Pleasant conversations and a state of harmony are within your capabilities today. This isn't just about expressing your feelings to those closest to you. Your positive disposition goes further than that in terms of your willingness to chat to almost anyone you come across. Be ready to seek advice from an older colleague or a relative.

18 WEDNESDAY ☿ *Moon Age Day 29   Moon Sign Cancer*

am ....

pm ....

With the Sun entering your solar fourth house this would be an ideal time to withdraw very slightly from the cut and thrust of everyday life and spend much more time thinking about home and family. You could do worse than to focus on the domestic scene if you want to get the very best from today, and it should help you to feel more secure.

19 THURSDAY ☿ *Moon Age Day 0   Moon Sign Cancer*

am ....

pm ....

Leisure activities enjoyed with your partner are favoured now, and to some extent you are encouraged to look ahead more than might have been the case earlier this week. In addition you have a chance to learn lessons from things that have gone before, so there's nothing wrong with allowing at least a small part of your mind to dwell in the past.

20 FRIDAY ☿ *Moon Age Day 1   Moon Sign Leo*

am ....

pm ....

This is a time of year for you, and one in which feeling appreciated by others counts for a great deal. You might tell the whole world that you don't really care whether others like you or not, but you can't fool your astrologer! Aries revels in being popular and loves to be loved. In social situations now you should be all smiles.

21 SATURDAY ☿ *Moon Age Day 2   Moon Sign Leo*

am ....

pm ....

Even if certain relationships are turning slightly more turbulent, you need to ask whether this is actually your fault. In most situations you merely need to monitor what is going on, and this probably isn't the ideal time for too much interference. Any arguments within the family are best avoided – that is, if you have any choice in the matter at all.

22 SUNDAY ☿ *Moon Age Day 3   Moon Sign Virgo*

am ....

pm ....

Why not take the opportunity today to alter routines to better suit prevailing circumstances? This could be at work, if you go to work on a Sunday, but is much more likely to relate to domestic issues. Changing family needs probably call for some reorganisation, and you could be just the person to sort things out.

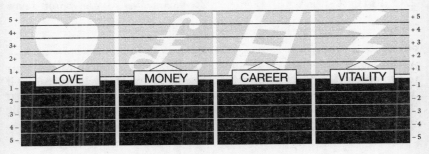

23 MONDAY ☿ *Moon Age Day 4 Moon Sign Virgo*

am ....

pm...

Love and romance are both well marked at the start of this particular July week. It's time to turn up the heat in your life, as is happening in the weather outside, and to make the most of the chance to tell someone how special they are. Even older Aries subjects can now be young at heart, and you might surprise yourself on a few occasions!

24 TUESDAY ☿ *Moon Age Day 5 Moon Sign Libra*

am ....

pm...

A few delays are possible while the lunar low is around, but if you retain your optimism and enthusiasm at this time you should be able to circumnavigate any real problems. If you really want to make the most of a less than inspiring two or three days you could choose to take a break and to go somewhere really beautiful.

25 WEDNESDAY ☿ *Moon Age Day 6 Moon Sign Libra*

am ....

pm...

Get plenty of rest and don't expect to do everything yourself. Better by far right now to supervise others and also to spend a few hours planning what you intend to do later. Even if people are relying on you, they can get by fine just as long as you are there to offer advice. This would not be a good time for taking unnecessary financial risks.

26 THURSDAY ☿ *Moon Age Day 7 Moon Sign Libra*

am ....

pm...

As the day wears on, so you should be able to sharpen your mind and start to see potential pitfalls before you arrive at them. Don't be surprised if not everyone believes you have the answers they need. You can only go so far in persuading others about anything, and in the end there some people who only learn through hard experience.

27 FRIDAY
☿   *Moon Age Day 8   Moon Sign Scorpio*

am ....

pm...

Difficulties are possible in relationships and even in your romantic life now that Mars is in your solar seventh house. Your best approach is to make sure you are very diplomatic when necessary. If you manage this, you should save yourself a number of unnecessary disputes or even arguments that only complicate situations.

28 SATURDAY
☿   *Moon Age Day 9   Moon Sign Scorpio*

am ....

pm...

Opportunities to get ahead today might have something to do with romance, or at the very least could involve a co-operative venture with a loved one. There are signs that you are tinged with genius right now when it comes to new notions, and it pays to listen carefully to what your inner mind is telling you. As always, you tend to act on instinct.

29 SUNDAY
☿ *Moon Age Day 10   Moon Sign Sagittarius*

am ....

pm...

You have scope to make new friends at this time, and if you do they may well be radically different from you in various ways. This is no bad thing. Staying alongside those who think and act exactly as you do can be tedious and sometimes counterproductive. Today is a chance to ring the changes.

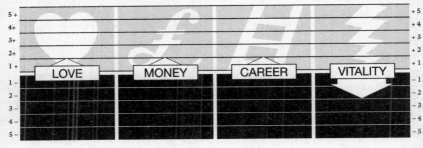

30 MONDAY   ☿ *Moon Age Day 11*   *Moon Sign Sagittarius*

am ....

pm ....

Business and practical matters come under the spotlight today. If you are forced to stay at home because of family commitments, there is much to be said for finding time to get some fresh air, even if it is only in your local park. On the other hand, if you are free to do whatever you like, this would be a favourable time to embark on a journey.

31 TUESDAY   ☿ *Moon Age Day 12*   *Moon Sign Capricorn*

am ....

pm ....

There is just a slight chance of disharmony breaking out within the family or in your social circle. It would be best if you avoided being a part of this, and where possible you need to play the honest broker. This might not be easy, but if you remain neutral people will respect you more in the longer term. Be ready to help out an older person today.

1 WEDNESDAY   ☿ *Moon Age Day 13*   *Moon Sign Capricorn*

am ....

pm ....

On the first day of August it may well occur to you that you haven't moved around as much this year as would sometimes be the case. You can address this by getting out and about, and maybe planning a holiday in the very near future. Your popularity counts for a great deal at this time, and you can positively shine in social situations.

2 THURSDAY   ☿ *Moon Age Day 14*   *Moon Sign Aquarius*

am ....

pm ....

Trends suggest that love has a part to play in your life now, even if you have not been particularly looking for it at this time. You also have what it takes to excel in social situations and if you are faced with having to talk in a public setting. Aries is now on top form. Make the most of the summer and of the chance to mix freely and move about.

3 FRIDAY
☿ *Moon Age Day 15   Moon Sign Aquarius*

am...

pm...

Capitalise on your ability to talk to almost anyone at this time. It doesn't matter who people are, or from what background they come. You have the ability to find something to say to them, and your egalitarian nature is particularly well emphasised at this time. Once again it looks as though travel is the order of the day.

4 SATURDAY
☿ *Moon Age Day 16   Moon Sign Pisces*

am...

pm...

The Moon in your solar twelfth house this weekend encourages a supersensitivity to atmospheres, making it less likely that you will decide to rush in where angels fear to tread, as is often the case for Aries. Diplomatic and flexible, you can make the best of impressions in any setting, especially if you can make yourself the focus of people's attention.

5 SUNDAY
☿ *Moon Age Day 17   Moon Sign Pisces*

am...

pm...

As a direct reversal to yesterday, there are signs of a slight tendency to bully certain people into doing what you want. It may not occur to you that this is what you are doing, unless you apply the more sensitive side of your nature again. Why not let those around you do what they feel is best, and do what you can to support them?

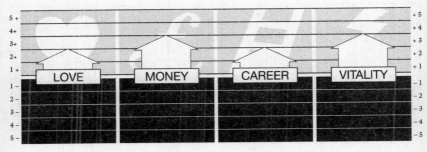

August

2012

Your Month at a Glance

⊕ = Opportunities are around ● = Be on the defensive ◯ = Life is pretty ordinary

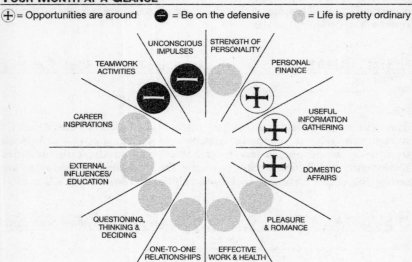

TEAMWORK ACTIVITIES

UNCONSCIOUS IMPULSES

STRENGTH OF PERSONALITY

PERSONAL FINANCE

CAREER INSPIRATIONS

USEFUL INFORMATION GATHERING

EXTERNAL INFLUENCES/ EDUCATION

DOMESTIC AFFAIRS

QUESTIONING, THINKING & DECIDING

PLEASURE & ROMANCE

ONE-TO-ONE RELATIONSHIPS

EFFECTIVE WORK & HEALTH

August Highs and Lows

Here I show you how the rhythms of the Moon will affect you this month. Like the tide, your energies and abilities will rise and fall with its pattern. When it is above the centre line, go for it, when it is below, you should be resting.

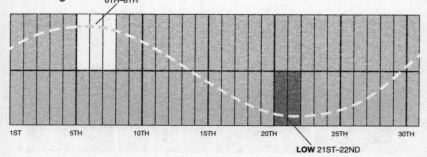

6TH–8TH

1ST   5TH   10TH   15TH   20TH   25TH   30TH

LOW 21ST–22ND

6 MONDAY ☿ *Moon Age Day 18   Moon Sign Aries*

am ....

pm ....

You should be able to get a great deal done today, and it all starts really early. With the lunar high around your energy levels are emphasised, and you might decide you want to be occupied from morning until night. There is also a positive focus on the social side of life, which is particularly good if you've chosen this week for a holiday.

7 TUESDAY ☿ *Moon Age Day 19   Moon Sign Aries*

am ....

pm ....

Energy should still be in plentiful supply, and you need to be ready to make the most of a wealth of new opportunities. Whilst others stand around and wonder what to do next, you can take any bull by the horns. Speaking of bulls, today's influences encourage friendly encounters with people born under the sign of Taurus – and also that of Virgo.

8 WEDNESDAY ☿ *Moon Age Day 20   Moon Sign Aries*

am ....

pm ....

For the third day running the Moon smiles down on you from your own zodiac sign, and that makes a hat-trick of days during which have scope to get more or less what you want from life. Part of your success is finding people around who think so much about you that they are willing to go to almost any length to keep you happy.

9 THURSDAY *Moon Age Day 21   Moon Sign Taurus*

am ....

pm ....

Intuitive insights are on offer from the present position of Mercury in your solar chart, and you should find it easy enough to put these into words. Don't expect everyone to appreciate what you are saying, and be prepared to explain yourself carefully. This could be difficult, particularly in situations that merely represent 'feelings'.

10 FRIDAY
Moon Age Day 22   Moon Sign Taurus

am ....

pm..

This is a time when you are encouraged to roam, perhaps with your partner, family members or friends. If you are lucky enough not to be at work today you could do something quite different and enjoy the change. Even if you can't get everyone on your side at first, when it matters the most you can get people to follow your lead.

11 SATURDAY
Moon Age Day 23   Moon Sign Gemini

am ....

pm..

Progress this weekend is a question of how you use your nervous energy, and there is much to be said for staying on the go. You certainly have what it takes to get plenty done and you are in a prime position to be of assistance to other people. If you feel slightly restless at home, it's worth thinking up some new little adventures.

12 SUNDAY
Moon Age Day 24   Moon Sign Gemini

am ....

pm..

An interesting and happy-go-lucky phase is inspired by the Sun in your solar fifth house, and your curiosity is also to the fore around now. Trends encourage you to leave no stone unturned when it comes to solving any puzzle that is currently on your mind, and you might even appear to some people to be slightly obsessive in one way or another.

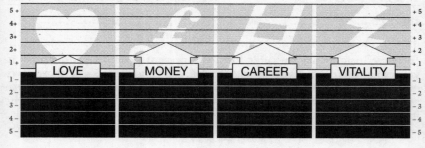

13 MONDAY   *Moon Age Day 25   Moon Sign Gemini*

am ....

pm...

A quieter and less demanding interlude is available, and this should give you the chance to catch up on a few things that have been put on the back burner so far this week. When dealing with younger family members it's important to find the time to really concentrate on what they are saying. This will help you to react in the right way.

14 TUESDAY   *Moon Age Day 26   Moon Sign Cancer*

am ....

pm...

Mercury now accentuates your powers of attraction, so if you have been looking for love, this is certainly a day to pay attention. Although it is quite possible that someone you never suspected is carrying a significant torch for you, it is in the direction of strangers that you are encouraged to look for most of this week.

15 WEDNESDAY   *Moon Age Day 27   Moon Sign Cancer*

am ....

pm...

Much can be achieved out here in the middle of the week if you use your energies wisely and concentrate on the task in hand. You can be extremely strong-willed at the moment, though of course there is nothing new about that. Despite your need to succeed, it's important to make sure that you are not trying to control other people.

16 THURSDAY   *Moon Age Day 28   Moon Sign Leo*

am ....

pm...

Your capacity to make the most of life's romantic interludes is becoming greater and greater. There is also much to be said for focusing on luxuries and physical pleasures of one sort or another during the Moon's present stay in your solar fifth house. Aries can be either very abstemious or quite hedonistic – and the latter is emphasised now.

17 FRIDAY

Moon Age Day 0   Moon Sign Leo

am ....

pm...

Rewards of a domestic sort remain within your reach as Venus continues its journey through your solar fourth house. Venturing far from home in order to find the happiness you seek may not be necessary because you are in a position to find most of what you are looking for either within your abode or close enough to the front door.

18 SATURDAY

Moon Age Day 1   Moon Sign Leo

am ....

pm...

A surge of renewed energy is on available today, and the sunny side of your nature should be on display for everyone to see. The spotlight is on finding happiness and fulfilment at this time, and if you can't do this, you are probably doing something slightly wrong. Take time out to smell the flowers as you dash around from one place to another.

19 SUNDAY

Moon Age Day 2   Moon Sign Virgo

am ....

pm...

Today is about remaining vital and enthusiastic. You are in the best possible position to benefit from opportunities that pass you by at breakneck speed. Such are your powers of perception at the moment that few people could fool you, and no situation should be beyond your powers of reasoning. You have a zest for life that is awe-inspiring.

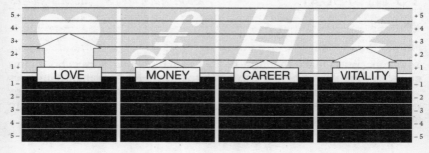

20 MONDAY

Moon Age Day 3   Moon Sign Virgo

am ....

pm ....

It pays to slow things down a little today because the lunar low is about to arrive, and if you enter it at speed it will be like hitting a brick wall. There are good reasons to spend a few hours today thinking things through and also talking to like-minded individuals. You don't have to stand still, but you could ease off somewhat.

21 TUESDAY

Moon Age Day 4   Moon Sign Libra

am ....

pm ....

Unrealistic expectations could cause you to feel somewhat lacking in success when they don't materialise. You need to ask yourself whether you have been truly realistic, and then get up and start again. For the moment the lunar low represents a constraining influence, which is all the more reason to enjoy the summer heat in a restful location.

22 WEDNESDAY

Moon Age Day 5   Moon Sign Libra

am ....

pm ....

When it comes to dealing with others on a one-to-one basis, tact and diplomacy are both needed, and unfortunately these could be in fairly short supply while the lunar low is around. It might be best to leave any planned confrontations until tomorrow or even after the weekend. In the meantime, remaining cool and calm is the order of the day.

23 THURSDAY

Moon Age Day 6   Moon Sign Scorpio

am ....

pm ....

Today is excellent for practical and rational thought. The Sun has now entered your solar sixth house, and in this position it assists you to discriminate well and encourages you to spend a few weeks sorting things out to your satisfaction and advantage. Your ability to work through situations is well accented – as is your diplomacy.

24 FRIDAY

Moon Age Day 7   Moon Sign Scorpio

am ....

pm..

You need to ask yourself whether you can continue everything in quite the same manner you did in the past. Change is part of the present planetary setup, but you need to ensure that it is well thought out and implemented carefully. The one thing you should avoid for the next day or two is a tendency to throw the baby out with the bathwater.

25 SATURDAY

Moon Age Day 8   Moon Sign Sagittarius

am ....

pm..

An ideal time to persuade others to put even more trust in you than they did before. This helps your ego, though you never had any doubt about your own integrity. With this greater trust comes more responsibility, but of a kind you should be quite happy to take on. You can afford to socialise as much as possible later in the day.

26 SUNDAY

Moon Age Day 9   Moon Sign Sagittarius

am ....

pm..

The potential looks positive, though what you might do to fully exploit it on a Sunday remains to be seen. There is nothing wrong with getting out there and enjoying yourself, and you might even decide to start a longer break. Be prepared to please your partner, and to keep your eyes wide open if you are looking for new love.

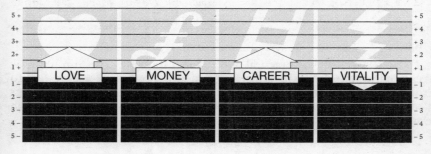

27 MONDAY   *Moon Age Day 10   Moon Sign Capricorn*

am ....

pm...

There are signs that a few tricky matters could develop in the professional arena, which is why it pays to keep your wits about you early this week. In the main you can respond to most situations quickly and decisively, which works well. Personal attachments cannot be treated in this way, because greater understanding is needed.

28 TUESDAY   *Moon Age Day 11   Moon Sign Capricorn*

am ....

pm...

You have a real talent for nurturing and assisting others, and although you sometimes keep this skill under wraps, using it now can really make the difference. This helps you to become the champion of the underdog, but also allows you to prove what a great teacher you are capable of being. Be ready to help a friend in trouble later.

29 WEDNESDAY   *Moon Age Day 12   Moon Sign Aquarius*

am ....

pm...

A carefree and easy-going approach works well for most of the time during the second part of this week, which is one of the reasons why it would be so fortunate if you happened to be on holiday at the moment. But even if you are not, you can use this interlude to lift the spirits of less positive people and to light any room, just by entering it.

30 THURSDAY   *Moon Age Day 13   Moon Sign Aquarius*

am ....

pm...

You thrive on competition at the best of times, but especially so now. It's natural to want to win in sporting situations, though you don't have to take this to extremes in terms of employing dubious strategies. It really is the case at the moment that it doesn't matter too much whether you win or lose. It is how you play the game that counts.

31 FRIDAY
Moon Age Day 14   Moon Sign Pisces

am ....

pm ....

Mercury in your solar fifth house enhances your charm and also highlights your artistic and aesthetic awareness. You have the ability today to make warm and potentially long-lasting contacts with some fascinating people. It's time to find individuals who are in a position to do you a great deal of good in the near future.

1 SATURDAY
Moon Age Day 15   Moon Sign Pisces

am ....

pm ....

The first day of September gives you a chance to show how much more relaxed and easy-going you can be at the moment. Working to strict plans is all very well, but you need to be prepared for defeat, and in many situations a slow and steady approach now works best. This isn't too much like Aries, but it is a good vacation.

2 SUNDAY
Moon Age Day 16   Moon Sign Pisces

am ....

pm ....

Confidence shouldn't be lacking, and you have everything you need to be right up there when it comes to making the best of impressions, especially on the social scene. This may not be a Sunday for trying to achieve anything material or concrete, though it is ideal for showing the world your true personality. It's time to scintillate!

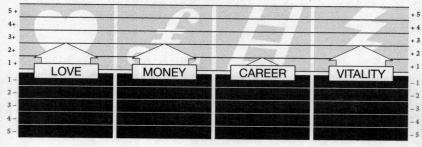

September 2012

YOUR MONTH AT A GLANCE

⊕ = Opportunities are around   ⊖ = Be on the defensive   ● = Life is pretty ordinary

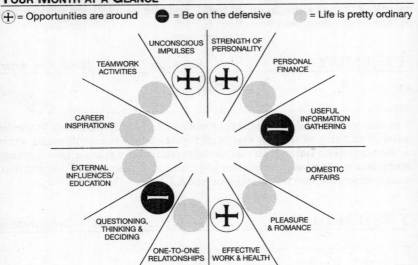

- UNCONSCIOUS IMPULSES ⊕
- STRENGTH OF PERSONALITY ⊕
- TEAMWORK ACTIVITIES
- PERSONAL FINANCE
- CAREER INSPIRATIONS
- USEFUL INFORMATION GATHERING ⊖
- EXTERNAL INFLUENCES/ EDUCATION
- DOMESTIC AFFAIRS
- QUESTIONING, THINKING & DECIDING ⊖
- ONE-TO-ONE RELATIONSHIPS
- EFFECTIVE WORK & HEALTH ⊕
- PLEASURE & ROMANCE

SEPTEMBER HIGHS AND LOWS

Here I show you how the rhythms of the Moon will affect you this month. Like the tide, your energies and abilities will rise and fall with its pattern. When it is above the centre line, go for it, when it is below, you should be resting.

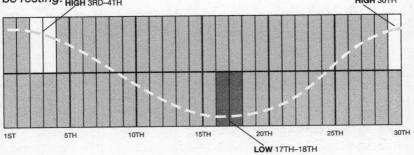

HIGH 3RD–4TH

HIGH 30TH

LOW 17TH–18TH

1ST   5TH   10TH   15TH   20TH   25TH   30TH

3 MONDAY
Moon Age Day 17   Moon Sign Aries

am ....

pm ....

This would be a great time to pull out all the guns. The start of September has potential to be very interesting for you, and it offers opportunities you probably didn't expect. The lunar high today means you can start the week in a very positive frame of mind, and you should have a good idea of how to get your own way.

4 TUESDAY
Moon Age Day 18   Moon Sign Aries

am ....

pm ....

You can now to take on new responsibilities, and you shouldn't be easily fazed by the sort of setback that might have caused you problems a week or two ago. The lunar high also assists you to be inspiring in company, which means you can have greater influence and can persuade others that your course of action is the right one to follow.

5 WEDNESDAY
Moon Age Day 19   Moon Sign Taurus

am ....

pm ....

Progress can now be made in all business affairs and there is a very practical feel to this part of the week. At the same time it's worth noticing that the year is advancing and that it won't be long before the weather starts to deteriorate. If there is something that needs doing out of doors, this might be a good time to tackle it.

6 THURSDAY
Moon Age Day 20   Moon Sign Taurus

am ....

pm ....

Ideas associated with business are still quite strongly highlighted, and even if you need to split your time between work and your social life, there are ways in which you can mix them successfully. Be prepared to do something you want to do later in the day and leave responsibilities alone for a while, especially this evening.

7 FRIDAY
Moon Age Day 21   Moon Sign Taurus

am ....

pm..

Even if you want to appear very much at ease today, there are signs that underneath a cool exterior you could be starting to niggle about something. Ask yourself whether it would be better to take decisive action, rather than mulling things over so much. There are times for Aries when it is best to wade in and do whatever seems most appropriate straight away.

8 SATURDAY
Moon Age Day 22   Moon Sign Gemini

am ....

pm..

Mars is now in your solar eighth house and there is no doubt that this can indicate an element of turmoil in your home life. Maybe you are thinking about making changes ahead of the winter, or perhaps you can't get loved ones to behave in what you consider an appropriate manner? Whatever the cause, remaining calm is the key.

9 SUNDAY
Moon Age Day 23   Moon Sign Gemini

am ....

pm..

Today offers scope for some pleasing moments on the romantic front, especially for young or young-at-heart Aries subjects. With new opportunities available to impress someone who is important to you, there's nothing to stop you speaking out on your own behalf. It's time to show how interesting and even fascinating you can be.

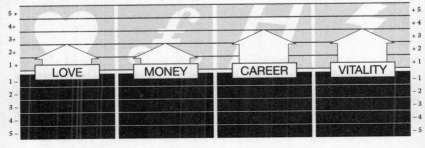

10 MONDAY
Moon Age Day 24   Moon Sign Cancer

am ....

pm...

With a good ability to sort out minor details, today should give you the chance to resolve matters you have found to be difficult in the past. Your strength now lies in your powers of reasoning, and you should be able to avoid making unforced errors in any of your dealings. Get a good early start for maximum success.

11 TUESDAY
Moon Age Day 25   Moon Sign Cancer

am ....

pm...

You now appreciate minor differences between the options available, and you can afford to be very exact in your dealings with the world. You need to be aware that you might appear fussy to some people, while others will simply smile. All the same, it's important to do things the way you know they should be done, even if others disagree.

12 WEDNESDAY
Moon Age Day 26   Moon Sign Cancer

am ....

pm...

You retain a good ability to see through situations and to weigh up the personalities of people around you almost instantly. Be careful though, because there's always a chance that you could be wrong. Where friends or business associates are concerned, there is much to be said for giving them the benefit of the doubt instead of overreacting.

13 THURSDAY
Moon Age Day 27   Moon Sign Leo

am ....

pm...

The Moon is now in your solar fifth house and this is a good planetary position for putting yourself in the spotlight and making a big impression without having to try too hard. You can be a real force for good in the world at the moment, and your popularity shouldn't be in doubt, especially when work is over and you are in social settings.

14 FRIDAY

Moon Age Day 28   Moon Sign Leo

am ....

pm..

A little more deliberation would be no bad thing, even if you have been in a pensive frame of mind for most of this week. Your interests are best served by staying on the right side of those in charge and by following their lead rather doing just what appeals to you. There are times when it's best to keep quiet, despite the fact that others are wrong.

15 SATURDAY

Moon Age Day 29   Moon Sign Virgo

am ....

pm..

Organised expansion into new areas can help you to further your aims this weekend. A serious-minded attitude is fine when it comes to money or practical matters, but you can afford be less intense when dealing with love or with your social life. Today can be a real split between doing things that are necessary and finding new ways to enjoy yourself.

16 SUNDAY

Moon Age Day 0   Moon Sign Virgo

am ....

pm..

With Mars so strong in your solar eighth house, this can be a time of dramatic change in some respects. A degree of renewal is indicated, and this could have a definite bearing on your personal life. If someone close to you is not taking you seriously, now is as good a time as any to let them know that you mean business.

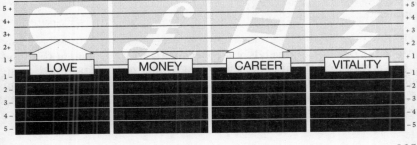

17 MONDAY
Moon Age Day 1   Moon Sign Libra

am ....

pm ....

Be ready to deal with a slight loss of confidence at the beginning of this week, but understand that it is very temporary and is merely one of the legacies of the lunar low. These are not the most fortunate trends for business, mainly because your mind could well be elsewhere. However, if you are willing to relax, today can be fine.

18 TUESDAY
Moon Age Day 2   Moon Sign Libra

am ....

pm ....

It's worth holding back on any really important decisions and deferring them until slightly later in the week. It isn't as if there are any really bad planetary trends around you, though it may be difficult to be quite so discriminating as usual. In any case, the Moon in Libra doesn't encourage you to look at the minutiae of situations.

19 WEDNESDAY
Moon Age Day 3   Moon Sign Scorpio

am ....

pm ....

There's nothing wrong today with focusing on having a good time rather than getting down to anything serious or demanding. The lunar low is out of the way, but a fifth-house Venus encourages you to leave consequences until a later date. It would not be wise to make any major changes to your life for a day or two.

20 THURSDAY
Moon Age Day 4   Moon Sign Scorpio

am ....

pm ....

Make the most of any friends and colleagues who are around at this time and capitalise on the support they will give for your plans. There is no doubt that you can get back in the driving seat, but that doesn't mean you can't still decide to enjoy yourself rather than get on with anything serious. It's up to you to create lots of laughs today.

21 FRIDAY

Moon Age Day 5   Moon Sign Sagittarius

am ....

pm..

Travelling and meeting people could seem quite exciting under present trends. There are important contacts to be made, particularly with certain individuals who could become increasingly important to you later on. This is an ideal time for meeting up with those who live at a distance, or even just for getting in touch, today or across the weekend.

22 SATURDAY

Moon Age Day 6   Moon Sign Sagittarius

am ....

pm..

Love life trends are well accented now, and with Venus in its present position you have a chance to show the person you love the most just how important they are to you. This can be achieved in a number of different ways, but however you go about it, make sure they are left in no doubt that your life would be very different without them.

23 SUNDAY

Moon Age Day 7   Moon Sign Capricorn

am ....

pm..

Co-operative affairs are positively highlighted at the moment, which is why today would be so good for addressing any issues to do with home and family. It's all about showing what good company you can be, and what a relaxed state of mind you are in. This would also be an ideal day for travelling, maybe to somewhere you haven't been before.

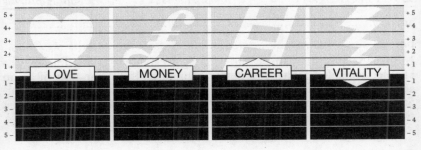

24 MONDAY
Moon Age Day 8   Moon Sign Capricorn

am ....

pm ....

This could be a time when you have scope to open the world up in some way. Perhaps you are being offered new options at work, or are looking around yourself in order to improve your lot in some way. Whatever you do today, it's worth approaching it in a spirit of enthusiasm and optimism. A positive start to the week.

25 TUESDAY
Moon Age Day 9   Moon Sign Aquarius

am ....

pm ....

If you find yourself under any sort of pressure as a result of the actions of those around you, this is a time when it pays to be slightly circumspect in the way you deal with matters. Aries is sometimes inclined to shoot from the hip, but to do so at the moment would probably not be the best approach. Seek out the warmth of friends.

26 WEDNESDAY
Moon Age Day 10   Moon Sign Aquarius

am ....

pm ....

Your social life is well starred as September begins to draw to its close. If you are willing to put concrete and practical matters on the back burner, you should be able to spend more time having fun and mixing with people you find both funny and stimulating. A particular new attraction could be encouraging you down slightly different roads.

27 THURSDAY
Moon Age Day 11   Moon Sign Aquarius

am ....

pm ....

Intimate relationships are favoured, and your ability to communicate with people probably hasn't been better all month. It's a question of being able to find just the right things to say at the most opportune moment. Stay away from contentious issues and other people's arguments. The last thing you need right now is to be over-serious.

28 FRIDAY
Moon Age Day 12   Moon Sign Pisces

am ....

pm..

Positive highlights now fall on creative and leisure-based matters, and you may decide to shelve practical issues until another day. You can't be expected to concentrate on the serious side of life all the time and you need to enjoy yourself, especially under present trends. Avoid pointless worries about matters you cannot possibly change.

29 SATURDAY
Moon Age Day 13   Moon Sign Pisces

am ....

pm..

Trends assist you to remain well balanced at the moment and to take a sensible view of life, as well as being able to address any issues that are troubling your friends. In romantic terms you should be giving, warm and very affectionate. Even if people try to draw you into discussions or arguments at this time, you don't have to take the bait!

30 SUNDAY
Moon Age Day 14   Moon Sign Aries

am ....

pm..

It is not a sin to sometimes think about yourself or what suits you, as you have a chance to find out today as the lunar high arrives. In any case, such is the concern in your nature at the moment that you are unlikely to take any action that works against the best interests of other people. Don't rule out a complete change of emphasis later today.

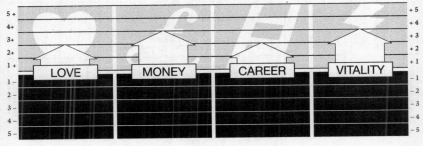

October

2012

YOUR MONTH AT A GLANCE

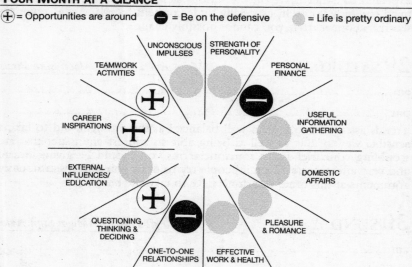

$\oplus$ = Opportunities are around $\ominus$ = Be on the defensive   = Life is pretty ordinary

UNCONSCIOUS IMPULSES

STRENGTH OF PERSONALITY

TEAMWORK ACTIVITIES

PERSONAL FINANCE

CAREER INSPIRATIONS

USEFUL INFORMATION GATHERING

EXTERNAL INFLUENCES/ EDUCATION

DOMESTIC AFFAIRS

QUESTIONING, THINKING & DECIDING

PLEASURE & ROMANCE

ONE-TO-ONE RELATIONSHIPS

EFFECTIVE WORK & HEALTH

OCTOBER HIGHS AND LOWS

Here I show you how the rhythms of the Moon will affect you this month. Like the tide, your energies and abilities will rise and fall with its pattern. When it is above the centre line, go for it, when it is below, you should be resting.

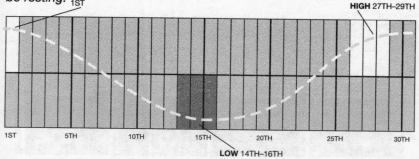

1ST

HIGH 27TH–29TH

1ST   5TH   10TH   15TH   20TH   25TH   30TH

LOW 14TH–16TH

1 MONDAY
Moon Age Day 15   Moon Sign Aries

am ....

pm..

It's the first day of October and you are up for something new and fresh. You have what it takes to make this a week that works to your advantage. The lunar high offers you much more energy and a slightly grittier 'edge' to your nature. If you make the most of the opportunities, things generally should be lining up well for you before today is out.

2 TUESDAY
Moon Age Day 16   Moon Sign Taurus

am ....

pm..

Personal satisfaction is emphasised under present trends, and there is much to be said for having an attitude that says 'If I am going to do something, I am going to do it right'. That's fine, but there could be other people around you at the moment who think slightly differently about things. You need to be both assertive and diplomatic.

3 WEDNESDAY
Moon Age Day 17   Moon Sign Taurus

am ....

pm..

Fulfilment is now possible in the form of one-to-one relationships. It's natural to wonder sometimes what the point is in being the most successful person in the world, if you don't have the time to share that success with someone close to you. For Aries it is possible to achieve both, but some forethought and careful planning is required.

4 THURSDAY
Moon Age Day 18   Moon Sign Taurus

am ....

pm..

You have scope to remain on the go from morning until night today, but might also be showing a great deal of curiosity regarding the way the world works. Keeping yourself mentally busy and physically active is fine, but you also need to understand the importance of stopping and taking stock, perhaps later in the day when you have time to relax.

5 FRIDAY

Moon Age Day 19   Moon Sign Gemini

am ....

pm...

A powerful period of change is at hand, even if you don't realise the fact in a moment-by-moment sense. With Mars in your solar eighth house this would be an ideal time to sort things out and get rid of items or ways of thinking that are no longer of any real use to you. Use some originality if you have to deal with wayward friends.

6 SATURDAY

Moon Age Day 20   Moon Sign Gemini

am ....

pm...

The Sun is presently in your solar seventh house and you can use the trends this brings to stay at the very centre of your social life. Keeping friends interested should be part of what you do, and at home it's worth making the effort to get on well with younger people. The relationships with the most potential today tend to be romantic ones.

7 SUNDAY

Moon Age Day 21   Moon Sign Cancer

am ....

pm...

There are good reasons to make this a quieter and less demanding sort of day, with the Moon in your solar fourth house and a great desire on your part to be at home and with your family. If you do travel today it's likely to be on short journeys, preferably in the company of people with whom you are truly at ease.

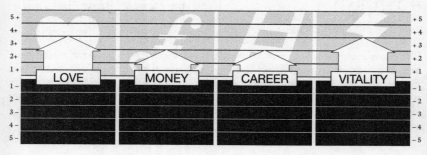

8 MONDAY
Moon Age Day 22   Moon Sign Cancer

am ....

pm ....

At this time you should be able to find out how much others are willing to defer to you, especially at work. If you make it clear to them that you know what you are doing, they are much more likely to follow your lead. Authority figures could also prove to be invaluable, particularly if you can persuade them to back your judgement.

9 TUESDAY
Moon Age Day 23   Moon Sign Cancer

am ....

pm ....

You now have scope to create greater warmth in your love life. This may be partly down to your willingness to offer more attention to the person who is really special in your life, which in turn relies on you realising how significant this individual is to you in so many ways. Aries can afford to be especially considerate under present trends.

10 WEDNESDAY
Moon Age Day 24   Moon Sign Leo

am ....

pm ....

Mars in your solar ninth house might encourage you to get yourself involved in some fairly fruitless arguments. You can best avoid this situation by taking care not to offer offence to anyone you think might be sensitive. Bulldozing your ideas is not to be recommended either.

11 THURSDAY
Moon Age Day 25   Moon Sign Leo

am ....

pm ....

Twosomes and joint endeavours generally are the way forward – that is, if you can get on with others well enough to achieve them. The more you co-operate today, the more smoothly things should go. Outside of work you have an opportunity to move away from routines and regimes, and should be looking instead for some variety and spontaneity.

12 FRIDAY

Moon Age Day 26   Moon Sign Virgo

am ....

pm..

It might be difficult to make much progress just at present, though Venus in your solar sixth house does assist you to bring some interest into relationships. The lunar low is on the way, and even now you may decide to slow certain matters to a snail's pace. Although this might not be ideal, they do say that patience is a virtue.

13 SATURDAY

Moon Age Day 27   Moon Sign Virgo

am ....

pm..

Despite quieter times you should still be able to come up with ideas, and this is assisted by the present position of Mars in your solar chart. Even if you can't move on in the way that you would wish, you can at least work out your strategies for later and sort out any necessary details well ahead of undertaking new enterprises.

14 SUNDAY

Moon Age Day 28   Moon Sign Libra

am..

pm..

The lunar low might sometimes take the wind out of your sails but if you have managed to cope during the last couple of days, you needn't allow this to be the case now. If life seems dull, by all means do something to pep it up, though pushing too hard can bring the risk of mistakes being made.

15 MONDAY

Moon Age Day 0   Moon Sign Libra

am ....

pm...

A day to pace yourself and stick to tried and tested paths to success. It might take time, and you will have to show a willingness to watch and wait, but you certainly have what it takes to get there in the end. Confidence could start to return as early as the end of today, but don't expect even the start of tomorrow to offer many startling opportunities.

16 TUESDAY

Moon Age Day 1   Moon Sign Libra

am ....

pm...

As the lunar low retreats, a more positive view of the future becomes possible, especially in terms of work. Meanwhile you can get the bit between your teeth regarding a journey or a new project. In terms of getting ahead both now and for the rest of this working week, it isn't so much what you know as who you know that counts.

17 WEDNESDAY

Moon Age Day 2   Moon Sign Scorpio

am ....

pm...

Be prepared to dig deep to get at the root of problems, particularly if they need to be solved before you can make progress. You need to consider whether those close to you are making the effort they should, and to offer encouragement at every stage if required. Romance should offer warmth and fulfilment now.

18 THURSDAY

Moon Age Day 3   Moon Sign Scorpio

am ....

pm...

Trends encourage you to enjoy a first-rate time socially and to make yourself the life and soul of any party that is taking place in your vicinity. This is not to suggest that you need to restrict yourself entirely to personal enjoyment. On the contrary, you should be willing to trade a good time for getting more done and achieving success.

19 FRIDAY
Moon Age Day 4   Moon Sign Sagittarius

am ....

pm...

People in positions of power and influence could now seem more approachable than they would have done around this time last week. Actually, the change is not in them but in you. Your strength at the moment lies in how you use your charm, and you shouldn't have any difficulty in finding the right words to both compliment and encourage.

20 SATURDAY
Moon Age Day 5   Moon Sign Sagittarius

am ....

pm...

Today is an opportunity to show that you are witty, and a veritable mine of information. Not all of what you know has to have a practical use. You can be quite funny, perhaps in a slightly scathing sort of way, but your ability to make others smile can be a useful quality in itself. Save time for personal attachments later today.

21 SUNDAY
Moon Age Day 6   Moon Sign Capricorn

am ....

pm...

The Moon in your solar tenth house strengthens your desire to succeed, though you might find it difficult to make any real headway on a Sunday. It would probably do you a great deal of good at this time to get out of the house and to find enjoyment alongside others who love nature at its most spectacular. Financial gains are within your reach.

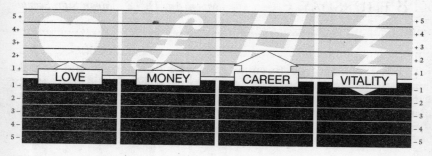

22 MONDAY
Moon Age Day 7   Moon Sign Capricorn

am ....

pm...

You can use communal activities to pep up your social life this week and to bring a breath of fresh air to any situations that have been getting rather stale in some way. Even if you can't win at everything you do today, you can at least make an impression, and that can be very useful, if not now, then at some time further down the road.

23 TUESDAY
Moon Age Day 8   Moon Sign Aquarius

am ....

pm...

Now it might be hard to hide feelings of warmth and friendliness – and why would you want to do so anyway? It's natural to feel that being very open leaves you somehow vulnerable, but this really isn't the case. Aries is a very astute zodiac sign and you always know how to protect yourself. Be ready to offer advice to a friend today.

24 WEDNESDAY
Moon Age Day 9   Moon Sign Aquarius

am ....

pm...

If you enjoy a challenge, as you undoubtedly do, today could allow you to create a lasting impression and a strong feeling of achievement. Routines are probably not for you at this time, and it pays to ring the changes at every opportunity. You can't expect everyone to be on your side at work, but you can gain support when you need it the most.

25 THURSDAY
Moon Age Day 10   Moon Sign Pisces

am ....

pm...

Right now circumstances are right for a job change or a move up the ladder of success. There are signs that you have been working especially hard of late, and this fact could well have been noticed. One of your main qualities is that you are conscientious, but at the same time you should realise how best to feather your own nest.

26 FRIDAY
Moon Age Day 11   Moon Sign Pisces

am ....

pm ....

Why not treat this as a day when you can escape reality for a short while? The Moon occupies your solar twelfth house today, just ahead of the lunar high. Today would be great for laying down plans, but is best of all for doing some dreaming. With some good application on your part, today's dreams could be tomorrow's realities.

27 SATURDAY
Moon Age Day 12   Moon Sign Aries

am ....

pm ....

The lunar high offers you new incentives and the ability to chase a few of your dreams all the way. You might not be able to use the lunar high this time for gains at work, but having the Moon in your zodiac sign at the weekend could give you the chance to show yourself at your best in social settings and in romantic clinches.

28 SUNDAY
Moon Age Day 13   Moon Sign Aries

am ....

pm ....

Certain endeavours offer an opportunity to prove how effective you can be, and you shouldn't have to work too hard to discover a pot of gold at the end of any rainbow. Getting down to brass tacks in family discussions clears the air, and if you are remain funny and diplomatic, you can probably get away with saying just about anything.

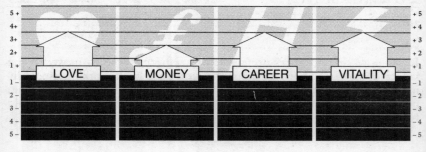

29 MONDAY
Moon Age Day 14   Moon Sign Aries

am ....

pm..

There is an intense focus on relationships with friends now that the Sun is in your solar eighth house, but you can also make this a time of change and a period when you have scope to get rid of things that don't suit you any more. With everything to play for in a financial sense, any investments you make now are particularly favoured.

30 TUESDAY
Moon Age Day 15   Moon Sign Taurus

am ....

pm..

Make plenty of room in your life for freedom of expression today, and spend as much time among other people as you can. This is not a good interlude for soldiering on alone or for locking yourself up in some secluded room. You can only shine when there are people to see you shining – otherwise all that effort is wasted.

31 WEDNESDAY
Moon Age Day 16   Moon Sign Taurus

am ....

pm..

There are signs that monetary stability could now be at the forefront of your mind, though with the potential to make so many changes at this time, you might find it somewhat difficult to keep track. If things are too complicated for you to understand, they must be really complicated! However, with patience you should soon understand.

1 THURSDAY
Moon Age Day 17   Moon Sign Gemini

am ....

pm..

It's important to make sure that others recognise your intelligence and your informed ideas. It's a question of ensuring you are smooth and concise in your thinking, talking and acting, and of instilling confidence in other people, even individuals you hardly know. Even a casual conversation at a bus stop could prove useful now – so keep listening.

2 FRIDAY
Moon Age Day 18   Moon Sign Gemini

am ....

pm ....

If you're feeling the need to break free from restrictions, that eighth-house Sun is now making itself felt quite strongly. The weekend lies ahead and you can afford to do something completely different if at all possible. You might be able to gain inspiration from family members, even those whose actions you don't particularly approve of.

3 SATURDAY
Moon Age Day 19   Moon Sign Gemini

am ....

pm ....

Be prepared for some exciting encounters today, some of which could occur so quickly and so unexpectedly you will have to be right on the ball to make the most of them. Look towards love this weekend because there are pleasant times for the taking. This is also an ideal opportunity to get to the root cause of any practical problems at home.

4 SUNDAY
Moon Age Day 20   Moon Sign Cancer

am ....

pm ....

There is a need for you to feel calm and secure in your personal feelings, and if anyone is upsetting you, this may not prove to be possible. Your best approach is to avoid rows, even ones that have nothing much to do with you. Opt instead for taking a seat on the edge of conflicts. In personal attachments you can be still warm and loving.

♈ November
2012

Your Month at a Glance

⊕ = Opportunities are around   ⊖ = Be on the defensive   ⬤ = Life is pretty ordinary

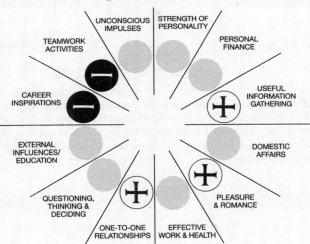

- UNCONSCIOUS IMPULSES
- STRENGTH OF PERSONALITY
- TEAMWORK ACTIVITIES
- PERSONAL FINANCE
- CAREER INSPIRATIONS
- USEFUL INFORMATION GATHERING
- EXTERNAL INFLUENCES/ EDUCATION
- DOMESTIC AFFAIRS
- QUESTIONING, THINKING & DECIDING
- PLEASURE & ROMANCE
- ONE-TO-ONE RELATIONSHIPS
- EFFECTIVE WORK & HEALTH

November Highs and Lows

Here I show you how the rhythms of the Moon will affect you this month. Like the tide, your energies and abilities will rise and fall with its pattern. When it is above the centre line, go for it, when it is below, you should be resting.

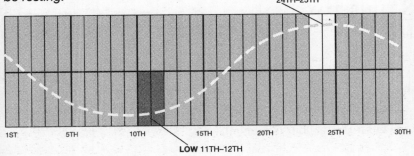

24TH–25TH

1ST   5TH   10TH   15TH   20TH   25TH   30TH

LOW 11TH–12TH

5 MONDAY
Moon Age Day 21   Moon Sign Cancer

am ....

pm..

Make the most of new opportunities today to do your own thing, and there is much to be said for putting travel high on your agenda. Don't be a stay-at-home this week, and make sure that you respond to any exciting offer that comes your way. The year may be getting older, but the advantages are increasing. Seek encouragement from friends.

6 TUESDAY
Moon Age Day 22   Moon Sign Leo

am ....

pm..

The emphasis on fun continues today, offering you scope to look for some real excitement and maybe the chance to pit yourself against a new challenge. It pays to make sure you stay in a really confident frame of mind, and to shrug off, if you can, any minor health difficulties that have surrounded you of late.

7 WEDNESDAY   ☿
Moon Age Day 23   Moon Sign Leo

am ....

pm..

The Sun remains in your solar eighth house, encouraging you to undertake a significant re-evaluation of your life. This would be an ideal time to make changes at home, and it isn't only your wardrobes and cupboards that are due for a sort out. Don't be afraid to dump old ideas as well, and replace them with newer and more exciting possibilities.

8 THURSDAY   ☿
Moon Age Day 24   Moon Sign Leo

am ....

pm..

When it comes to getting ahead generally you now have an opportunity to show a great deal more ingenuity and to turn your radar in the direction of quite significant alterations to your working and maybe also your social life. If you don't relish outside interference right now, be prepared to be firm and make up your own mind.

9 FRIDAY ☿ *Moon Age Day 25   Moon Sign Virgo*

am ....

pm...

Trends suggest that your mind should now be working like lightning, allowing you to bring new incentives even closer to reality and to make split-second decisions. If there are jobs to do today that you don't care for, why not get these out of the way as early in the day as possible? That way you leave the decks free for more concerted actions later.

10 SATURDAY ☿ *Moon Age Day 26   Moon Sign Virgo*

am ....

pm...

This is the last day before the lunar low, so it's worth keeping up the pace as much as possible. At the same time you need to realise that the second part of the weekend works best if you opt for a much quieter interlude than today. In some ways it's a natural process, and you might even decide to slow your mind and relax by this evening.

11 SUNDAY ☿ *Moon Age Day 27   Moon Sign Libra*

am ....

pm...

There is much to be said for making this a steady and reflective sort of Sunday and for not entertaining too many new ideas or strenuous pastimes. The lunar low is ideal for spending time with family members and whiling away a few hours doing interesting but not too demanding activities. Periods of rest are important, even for Aries subjects.

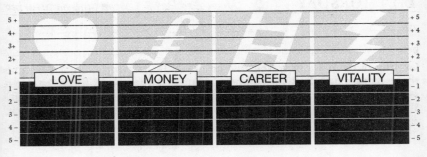

12 MONDAY ☿ *Moon Age Day 28   Moon Sign Libra*

am ....

pm ....

You can afford to be slightly more ambitious about plans and schemes at the start of this particular week, though there are good reasons for deferring your return to a frenetic pace until Wednesday. For now you can take time out to look at ideas without having to implement them straight away. Financial gains could be there for the taking.

13 TUESDAY ☿ *Moon Age Day 0   Moon Sign Scorpio*

am ....

pm ....

Do you feel that you are not getting the opportunities you would wish to put across your point of view in the way you really want to do? Make sure that the most important people are listening to what you have to say, and if necessary be prepared to repeat yourself. Socially speaking you now have scope to find contentment.

14 WEDNESDAY ☿ *Moon Age Day 1   Moon Sign Scorpio*

am ....

pm ....

Once again that eighth-house Sun encourages to you assess whether certain situations have run their course, and you could still be in the middle of an 'off with the old and on with the new' period. Some care is necessary, since you need to avoid getting rid of things now that still have some importance and also some use.

15 THURSDAY ☿ *Moon Age Day 2   Moon Sign Sagittarius*

am ....

pm ....

Getting out and about is well advised now. OK, so winter has arrived and there could be chilly winds blowing, but it is very good for you to get some fresh air and to blow away the cobwebs – more so now than usual. With everything to play for in a work situation, staying on the ball is what today is all about.

16 FRIDAY
☿ *Moon Age Day 3* *Moon Sign Sagittarius*

am ....

pm...

Now is definitely a time to act on your convictions, even if these sometimes go against the wishes or desires of those around you. On those occasions when you are absolutely certain that you are correct in your judgement, you shouldn't be afraid to act. If necessary you can explain yourself later but there may not be time to do so immediately.

17 SATURDAY
☿ *Moon Age Day 4* *Moon Sign Capricorn*

am ....

pm...

Diplomatic niceties are all well and good, but you are still in a position where changes have to be made, and the Sun only remains in your solar eighth house for a few more days. After that it's important to settle back down to routines. As long as you don't deliberately set out to upset anyone, you should be able to cope with repercussions.

18 SUNDAY
☿ *Moon Age Day 5* *Moon Sign Capricorn*

am ....

pm...

Be prepared to look out for love, exciting romance and some unexpected but positive happenings. You can make today really exciting, even if you're not expecting it to be so as the day gets started. It's a question of responding to changes in situations, especially in terms of relationships. You might even find others developing a brand new attitude.

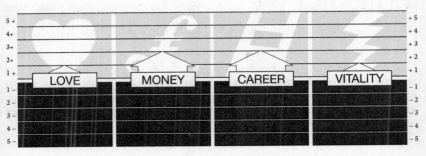

19 MONDAY ☿ *Moon Age Day 6 Moon Sign Aquarius*

am ....

pm ....

The spotlight is now on your desire to get through the superficialities of situations and to get to the heart of matters as soon as you can. This is particularly true at work, and you might not be too keen to sit around and discuss things endlessly. Certainly it pays to explain yourself, but after that you need to be up and running.

20 TUESDAY ☿ *Moon Age Day 7 Moon Sign Aquarius*

am ....

pm ....

A day to reach out and make as much contact with people as proves to be possible. The Sun is changing its position in your solar chart, encouraging you to be slightly less assertive and frenetic than you have been. Socialising is important at present, particularly if you decide to get together with friends you don't see too often.

21 WEDNESDAY ☿ *Moon Age Day 8 Moon Sign Pisces*

am ....

pm ....

Don't be surprised if others seem quite opposed to your ideas at the moment. Your best approach is to persuade them carefully that you know what you are talking about. Attitude is also important when it comes to your love life. Being reasonable with your partner can work wonders, and you need to show that you are really listening to them.

22 THURSDAY ☿ *Moon Age Day 9 Moon Sign Pisces*

am ....

pm ....

Social and business gatherings are favoured now, and you are in a position to intermix them a great deal. On a personal footing this would be an ideal opportunity to reach an understanding with someone close to you. You can help this process by continuing to take life steadier and by not being in any sort of rush.

23 FRIDAY ☿ *Moon Age Day 10   Moon Sign Pisces*

am ....

pm...

Be prepared to make this a quieter sort of day as the Moon passes through your solar twelfth house. By tomorrow it can be 'situation normal' again, but for the moment you can afford to watch and wait. Patience is not generally your best virtue, but there are good reasons for relaxing and waiting for things to mature before you act.

24 SATURDAY ☿ *Moon Age Day 11   Moon Sign Aries*

am ....

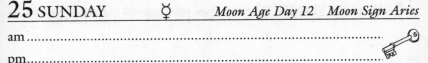

pm...

A steady growth is on offer, but so is your usual desire to get things moving. With the lunar high arriving at the weekend you may choose to make more of your life away from the practicalities of work and to find something exciting to do. Both money matters and your level of general good luck are now highlighted to a much greater extent.

25 SUNDAY ☿ *Moon Age Day 12   Moon Sign Aries*

am ....

pm...

Energy levels remain high, and even though this is a Sunday you needn't sit around waiting for life to come to you today. Vitality is the name of the game, though this could easily turn to restlessness unless you keep moving and acting. Speaking of acting, you have what it takes to be all things to all people under present trends.

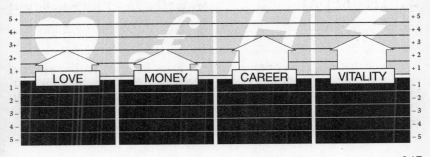

26 MONDAY ☿ *Moon Age Day 13 Moon Sign Taurus*

am..

pm..

Things should settle down nicely today, or at least they would if it were not for that Aries tendency to want the personal freedom to do what you wish at every level. On the one hand you are willing to watch and wait but on the other you have to keep tampering and interfering. The result could be a definite mixed bag.

27 TUESDAY ☿ *Moon Age Day 14 Moon Sign Taurus*

am..

pm..

If you are intent on concentrating on hard work now, you probably won't have too much time to watch what other people are doing or to keep assisting them. It's natural to find routines to be a real drag, and you will be much happier when situations keep changing. Beware of running yourself ragged – that won't be much of a help.

28 WEDNESDAY *Moon Age Day 15 Moon Sign Taurus*

am..

pm..

All close affairs and romantic attachments look well starred, thanks to the present position of Venus. However, this influence also encourages you to want to make changes of emphasis in personal relationships, which might not suit others as much as they do you. Sporting activity is also highlighted under present trends, but don't go overboard!

29 THURSDAY *Moon Age Day 16 Moon Sign Gemini*

am..

pm..

Anything that has been unsatisfactory in your life now needs sweeping away and replacing with newer and more positive actions on your part. Even if you can't have everything you want, all at the same time, you can at least make a start. Slow and steady wins most races, though it doesn't always seem so to Aries.

30 FRIDAY
Moon Age Day 17   Moon Sign Gemini

am...

pm...

An ideal time to consider a change of career, or to make significant alterations with regard to your present job. Some of what happens might be beyond your own control, but in a general sense you have what it takes to make progress. Be ready to welcome new personalities into your life at any time now, and especially across the weekend.

1 SATURDAY
Moon Age Day 18   Moon Sign Cancer

am...

pm...

Home and family count for a great deal today, particularly if you feel you haven't given quite enough time to such considerations during a busy week. Attention to detail is vital when it comes to new hobbies, but you might also decide to exploit the very active and sporting side of your nature under current influences.

2 SUNDAY
Moon Age Day 19   Moon Sign Cancer

am...

pm...

Trends offer you very wide horizons now, and spending a few hours today exploring your potential for the future can make all the difference. The year might be old, but you can be brand new in your thinking and your willingness to forge new paths. Any small obstacles are best dealt with one at a time and without any great rush.

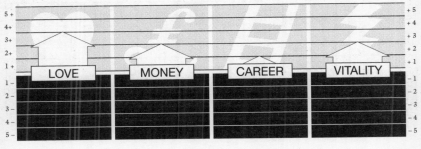

December 2012

YOUR MONTH AT A GLANCE

⊕ = Opportunities are around ● = Be on the defensive ● = Life is pretty ordinary

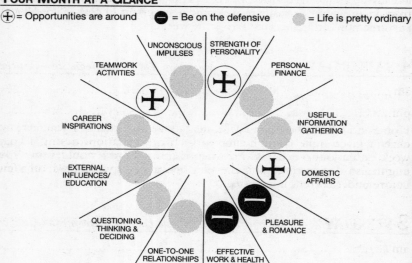

UNCONSCIOUS IMPULSES
STRENGTH OF PERSONALITY
TEAMWORK ACTIVITIES
PERSONAL FINANCE
CAREER INSPIRATIONS
USEFUL INFORMATION GATHERING
EXTERNAL INFLUENCES/ EDUCATION
DOMESTIC AFFAIRS
QUESTIONING, THINKING & DECIDING
PLEASURE & ROMANCE
ONE-TO-ONE RELATIONSHIPS
EFFECTIVE WORK & HEALTH

DECEMBER HIGHS AND LOWS

Here I show you how the rhythms of the Moon will affect you this month. Like the tide, your energies and abilities will rise and fall with its pattern. When it is above the centre line, go for it, when it is below, you should be resting.

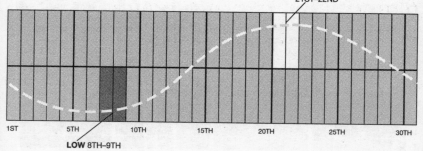

21ST–22ND

1ST   5TH   10TH   15TH   20TH   25TH   30TH

LOW 8TH–9TH

3 MONDAY

Moon Age Day 20   Moon Sign Cancer

am ....

pm ....

You have what it takes to make yourself the centre of attention in all social situations and to turn heads wherever you go. Many Aries subjects will already be in Christmas mode, and this would be an ideal time to start planning for some very special events that are going to come slightly later in the month.

4 TUESDAY

Moon Age Day 21   Moon Sign Leo

am ....

pm ....

Career-wise you are suited to almost any job that offers you a significant challenge, though you might be rather bored at the moment if your working life is not offering you the stimulation you would wish. The emphasis now is on getting on, even if that requires you to take on a few confrontations.

5 WEDNESDAY

Moon Age Day 22   Moon Sign Leo

am ....

pm ....

Strength of will now comes from situations in which you pit yourself against the world at large. Some of these happenings are of your own choosing, and will give you an opportunity to look back on what you have done and to realise how much your success lay in your own hands. The competitive side of your nature is to the fore just now.

6 THURSDAY

Moon Age Day 23   Moon Sign Virgo

am ....

pm ....

Close emotional involvements could now prove more satisfying than ever. It's natural to want to let others know your true feelings from time to time, and although a little patience may be necessary, you can usually get your message across. You can't expect everyone to be rooting for you at present, but can persuade those who matter the most to do so.

7 FRIDAY

Moon Age Day 24   Moon Sign Virgo

am ....

pm ....

When it comes to the everyday business of living your life, be prepared to identify a range of people who can be of assistance. Some of these individuals may not be well known to you, though the sheer warmth of your nature at this time helps you to attract their attention. Make the most of social encounters today – and keep moving.

8 SATURDAY

Moon Age Day 25   Moon Sign Libra

am ....

pm ....

You can afford to settle for a fairly quiet sort of Saturday. The lunar low is around, encouraging you to spend moments alone, perhaps with a good book. Nevertheless, the more you are in the company of loved ones, the greater should be your feelings of satisfaction. This might not be the best of days for travelling too far.

9 SUNDAY

Moon Age Day 26   Moon Sign Libra

am ....

pm ....

Beware of potential setbacks today, but instead of shying away from them, meet them head-on. This is not usually the best advice for the time of the lunar low, but you do have some very strong planetary positions to call upon at the moment. It isn't direct conflict that works best though, but a solid and quiet determination to keep going.

10 MONDAY   *Moon Age Day 27   Moon Sign Scorpio*

am ....

pm ....

Social issues have little going for them today, so you may decide that it is more sensible to turn your attention towards practicalities instead. At work you have scope to be progressive and even dynamic. It shouldn't be long before you are giving the whole world and his dog advice of the sort that Aries people find easy to dispense.

11 TUESDAY   *Moon Age Day 28   Moon Sign Scorpio*

am ....

pm ....

It's worth making certain you are aware of the motives of others at this time, particularly those who have some sort of interest in pulling the wool over your eyes. There are gains to be made from keeping a high profile in company, and from refusing to be put off by pessimistic individuals. It's time for you to become a guiding force.

12 WEDNESDAY   *Moon Age Day 0   Moon Sign Sagittarius*

am ....

pm ....

Planetary aspects being what they are, love and romance bring out the best in you now. Why not turn aside from the practical necessities of life and look carefully at your partner? Aries people who are in the market for a new relationship can capitalise on the fact that present trends should favour them more than has been the case of late.

13 THURSDAY   *Moon Age Day 1   Moon Sign Sagittarius*

am ....

pm ....

The real enjoyment in your life today is most likely to be found in and around your home. This could well remain the case until a good deal later in the month. There is much to be said for persuading relatives to do you favours. More importantly, you can gain so much more than usual from intimate contacts, and you should be in the market for affection.

14 FRIDAY
Moon Age Day 2   Moon Sign Capricorn

am ....

pm...

It looks as though a period of potential financial improvement is on offer. This is obviously a positive thing so close to Christmas. Part of the situation depends upon you looking carefully at your own money, and seeing how you can rationalise some spending. In the end it's about making sure you are better off than you were.

15 SATURDAY
Moon Age Day 3   Moon Sign Capricorn

am ....

pm...

If you make sure you add some positive thinking to the weekend, you stand the best chance of getting it to go with a swing. Be prepared to turn your mind to Christmas, which, after all, is not too far away. Prior planning isn't always your thing, but it is necessary sometimes. Are there any family birthdays or anniversaries you should have remembered?

16 SUNDAY
Moon Age Day 4   Moon Sign Aquarius

am ....

pm...

It looks as though you can afford to test your luck today because it is highly unlikely to let you down. Routines could be something of a bind, and there's nothing wrong with avoiding them if you possibly can. Meanwhile you can push forward progressively, and might already be enjoying the social side of Christmas.

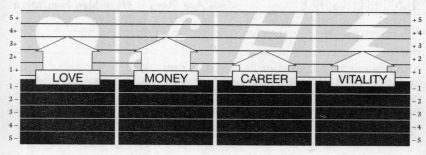

17 MONDAY
Moon Age Day 5   Moon Sign Aquarius

am ....

pm ....

The emphasis you wish to place on material and professional plans now receives a very definite boost. Making an early start is the best way of getting on top of things quickly. Once again, routines are probably for the birds as you move forward positively into areas of life that fascinate you and which prove successful.

18 TUESDAY
Moon Age Day 6   Moon Sign Aquarius

am ....

pm ....

For today at least you have scope to sit back and allow domestic matters to take care of themselves. This is one way of proving to yourself that it is possible for you to interfere too much right now. Getting others to do what you want at work can make all the difference, and routine financial transactions have a great deal to offer.

19 WEDNESDAY
Moon Age Day 7   Moon Sign Pisces

am ....

pm ....

It isn't unusual for you, but standing out in a crowd should be a natural aspect of life now, as you can definitely benefit from a boost to your ego. It pays to avoid family arguments, which cannot help you in any way at the moment, and to take a generally optimistic view of life. Give yourself chance to relax, once the daily round is over.

20 THURSDAY
Moon Age Day 8   Moon Sign Pisces

am ....

pm ....

With Christmas in view, high spirits should be to the fore, and you can welcome back the sense of joy that is so important to your zodiac sign. You shouldn't be surprised if not everyone is as happy as you are today, but you do have the capacity to cheer up others if you put your mind to it. Personal issues demand a matter-of-fact attitude at present.

21 FRIDAY
Moon Age Day 9   Moon Sign Aries

am...

pm...

It won't take long to realise that the lunar high arrives today, assisting you to add extra oomph to your life and encouraging a 'party' state of mind that might not have really been present so far this Christmas time. It takes people with real energy to keep up with you, and it pays to mix with those who hold similar values to your own.

22 SATURDAY
Moon Age Day 10   Moon Sign Aries

am...

pm...

You are in a position to accomplish a great deal around now, and shouldn't have much difficulty in persuading people to go along with your ideas. It's worth interrupting the flow of festivities to put your practical head on and turn your thoughts towards work, whether or not you are actually there at the weekend.

23 SUNDAY
Moon Age Day 11   Moon Sign Taurus

am...

pm...

Remaining on the go is what today is all about, and you could find the possibility of any sort of travel to be quite exciting. Trends suggest less of an inclination to stay in one spot in any case, and you might even decide to brave the crowds to do some last-minute Christmas shopping. Make sure a general sense of goodwill pervades your life now.

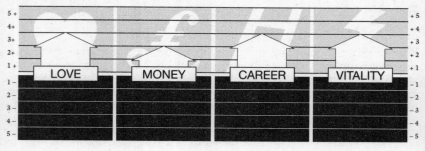

24 MONDAY   *Moon Age Day 12   Moon Sign Taurus*

am ....

pm..

Your ability to enjoy conversation should be there for all to see, and even gossip isn't beneath you on this Christmas Eve. Quality time spent with loved ones can also offer enjoyment, and may be an opportunity to discover things about yourself that have been a mystery up to now. It's time to create a warm and happy atmosphere for those close to you.

25 TUESDAY   *Moon Age Day 13   Moon Sign Taurus*

am ....

pm..

There is no reason at all why you shouldn't be able to enjoy Christmas Day, though it might not be quite as riotous as the days that follow it. A family time would suit you best of all, and that may well be what you are planning in any case. Vitality levels should improve as the day goes on.

26 WEDNESDAY   *Moon Age Day 14   Moon Sign Gemini*

am ....

pm..

The emphasis is on your self-reliance on this Boxing Day, though you need to bear in mind that other people might find this difficult to deal with. Your best approach is to stay away from anyone who seems determined to cause trouble and find a path through your own social life that fits your own needs. Family matters are to the fore today.

27 THURSDAY   *Moon Age Day 15   Moon Sign Gemini*

am ....

pm..

Your ability to attain the good things in life, and especially money, is noteworthy now. Take whatever direction is necessary in order to get ahead, stopping short only of treading on the toes of others. Socially speaking, the kindest side of your Aries nature should now be clearly on display. Make sure you are enjoying your presents.

28 FRIDAY

Moon Age Day 16   Moon Sign Cancer

am...

pm...

Trends assist you to obtain a positive response today, not only from your partner and people you know, but also from strangers. The focus is on your willingness to share, and to offer the benefit of your experience.

29 SATURDAY

Moon Age Day 17   Moon Sign Cancer

am...

pm...

The party animal within you remains quite evident, but it should also be possible for you to enjoy some quiet spells today, influenced by the position of the Moon in your solar chart.

30 SUNDAY

Moon Age Day 18   Moon Sign Cancer

am...

pm...

You need to avoid being too extravagant today. Spending money you don't actually possess is not to be recommended, and it can lead to a few worries at the very end of the year, or into next January.

31 MONDAY

Moon Age Day 19   Moon Sign Leo

am...

pm...

Make sure a sense of freedom and lightness of touch predominates on this New Year's Eve. Even if you aren't exactly in the mood to party until dawn, that needn't stop you from mixing with people. You can make today quite fascinating in a number of ways.

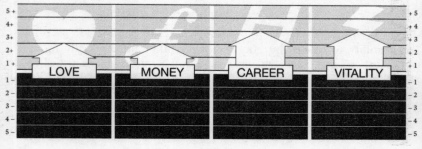

RISING SIGNS FOR ARIES

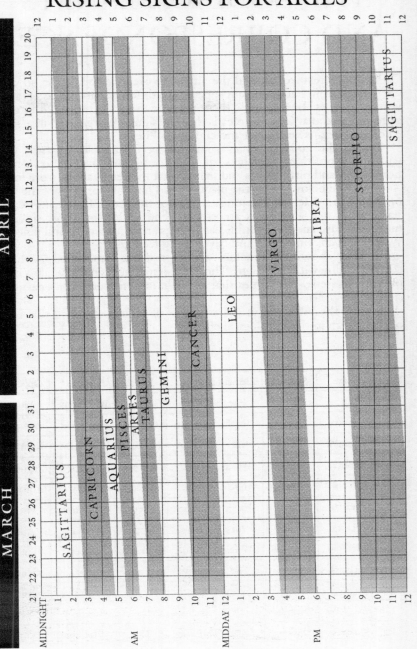

THE ZODIAC, PLANETS AND CORRESPONDENCES

The Earth revolves around the Sun once every calendar year, so when viewed from Earth the Sun appears in a different part of the sky as the year progresses. In astrology, these parts of the sky are divided into the signs of the zodiac and this means that the signs are organised in a circle. The circle begins with Aries and ends with Pisces.

Taking the zodiac sign as a starting point, astrologers then work with all the positions of planets, stars and many other factors to calculate horoscopes and birth charts and tell us what the stars have in store for us.

The table below shows the planets and Elements for each of the signs of the zodiac. Each sign belongs to one of the four Elements: Fire, Air, Earth or Water. Fire signs are creative and enthusiastic; Air signs are mentally active and thoughtful; Earth signs are constructive and practical; Water signs are emotional and have strong feelings.

It also shows the metals and gemstones associated with, or corresponding with, each sign. The correspondence is made when a metal or stone possesses properties that are held in common with a particular sign of the zodiac.

Finally, the table shows the opposite of each star sign – this is the opposite sign in the astrological circle.

Placed	Sign	Symbol	Element	Planet	Metal	Stone	Opposite
1	Aries	Ram	Fire	Mars	Iron	Bloodstone	Libra
2	Taurus	Bull	Earth	Venus	Copper	Sapphire	Scorpio
3	Gemini	Twins	Air	Mercury	Mercury	Tiger's Eye	Sagittarius
4	Cancer	Crab	Water	Moon	Silver	Pearl	Capricorn
5	Leo	Lion	Fire	Sun	Gold	Ruby	Aquarius
6	Virgo	Maiden	Earth	Mercury	Mercury	Sardonyx	Pisces
7	Libra	Scales	Air	Venus	Copper	Sapphire	Aries
8	Scorpio	Scorpion	Water	Pluto	Plutonium	Jasper	Taurus
9	Sagittarius	Archer	Fire	Jupiter	Tin	Topaz	Gemini
10	Capricorn	Goat	Earth	Saturn	Lead	Black Onyx	Cancer
11	Aquarius	Waterbearer	Air	Uranus	Uranium	Amethyst	Leo
12	Pisces	Fishes	Water	Neptune	Tin	Moonstone	Virgo